Marriage Is for Life

No Broken Promises, No Shattered Dreams

by Reverend Albert B. Wingfield

CTS Family Press • Fort Wayne

Scripture quotations from the New International Version,
1984, Zondervan Bible Publishers. Used by permission.
Pictures courtesy of Viking Photography. Used by permission.

Library of Congress Card Catalog Number: 99-069844

ISBN 1-930260-03-2

This book is dedicated

To my wife, Marge, who agreed to become my bride 46 years ago, when she was just 17 years old and I was 19. Church and family have always been our focus.

To our children and grandchildren, who have brought great joy and pleasure into our lives.

To the many faithful pastors and teachers who hold to the Biblical principals that "Marriage Is for Life."

A special word of thanks to The Rev. Dr. Dean O. Wenthe, The Rev. Dr. Alvin L. Barry, Rev. David Mommens and Deaconess Pamela Nielsen for their kind words.

Thanks also to Trudy Behning and Lisa Ramey for their help in proofreading the manuscript and typsetting the book.

Table of Contents

1   Reading This Book 1

2   Communication, Communication, Communication! .17

3   God's Word, Will and Rule 41

4   Accusation, Criticism and Blame 63

5   Children in a Troubled Marriage 83

6   A New Beginning 99

7   Lo, I Am With You, Each Day at a Time 115

8   Running Together 131

    For Engaged Couples 141

    Forgiveness After Divorce 143

❀ Chapter 1 ❀
Reading the Book

C hances are if you are reading this book, it is because you have loved ones who have a troubled marriage, you have a troubled marriage or you want to use this book as a resource to help a troubled marriage. Whatever your reason, I am writing this book in hopes that it can be used to put hurting couples in touch with each other in a way that their marriage can be healed or for couples planning to be married.

I am writing this book because I heard a little girl say, "I wish my mommy and daddy would not fuss. I love them. I wish we could just be a happy family."

I am writing this book for Amy Jo. Her mommy and daddy verbally and physically abused her at times because of their own hurt and pain.

I am writing this book for Anna. She said, "Please help Bill and me. We verbally abuse one another in front of our children so much, they really do not have much of a life at all. I guess we will have to divorce, I really see no other way, but this is sure not what I thought my marriage would be like."

This book was written to help heal a troubled marriage and to help newly married or engaged couples to avoid problems that may lead to troubled relationships.

1

Marriage Is for Life!

Couples of all ages, in all walks of life, are having their lives shattered, their children scarred for life because their marriages have broken down. They have tried to make it through and there just seems to be absolutely no way out.

Mark is a 32-year-old business man. He and his beautiful wife Mary, 31, have been married for ten years and have two lovely children; Mark Andrew is five and Chelsie is two.

Mark put it this way with tears in his eyes. "I tried so hard, worked two jobs to buy the house. We wanted a four bedroom home on two acres in the country. We got it. Mary had to work. Things started to happen. We talked to the pastor and he recommended a counselor. I felt like he put too much of the blame on me. I would not go back. I love my children and I think I still love Mary, but I guess we will just go our separate ways. It is just not worth the hassle. I feel like a failure at 32 years old. There is not much left to look forward to right now."

Mary says Mark spends more time at the neighborhood bar when he gets off work than he does at home with her and the children.

"Mark has been a good provider but I have had to work to make ends meet. I am just tired of all the fussing we do and I guess I really do not care any longer. Then I think, but what about the children? I feel so alone; I am a failure. Where is God? I just wanted a happy home, a loving husband and healthy children. I have nothing to look forward to. Where did we go wrong?"

What happens when a marriage goes sour for any reason? Is it possible to get help? Where can people turn?

I hope this book will provide an opportunity for each one of you who needs help to start on God's road to healing your marriage.

I am also writing this book in honor of my own wife, Marge, who has been married to me for 46 years. The Lord has blessed us with six children: Robert, Phillip, Linda, Judy, Carol and Rebecca. We are also blessed with 16 grandchildren. We have never thought of divorce as an option in our marriage, nor do we believe that it is today.

We live in a world that promotes divorce—if it is not working get out of the situation.

America and many other countries are losing the central core of their mainstay—one woman, one man, till death do us part. If we do not save our families by healing and saving marriages in trouble, we lose the wife, the husband and the children to a much less meaningful and enjoyable life. Furthermore, society loses the stability that a solid marriage gives.

Help! What Is Wrong?

Here are some examples we must face in the world in which we live. Many American families are falling apart. Divorce, even among the clergy, increases. More than a million children are murdered each year by abortion. Chastity and commitment to marriage do not get high marks from modern America.

In a study conducted at the University of California in Irvine, a team of social psychologists found that among Asian-American women, individuals from the least acculturated families were more likely to be virgins (77%) than were those from moderately or highly acculturated families (52% and 53% respectively).

The sexual morals now prevalent in the dominant American culture may be inferred from the fact that the average young Caucasian woman in this study reported having had 2.50 sexual partners compared to just 0.92 among the young Asian-American women.

In a study conducted at Arizona State University of Mexican-American young women, researchers found that those most fully assimilated into the dominant culture were those most likely to be pregnant outside wedlock.

The point? These young people learned to follow the morals of the host country, America. In 1972, 21% of adults surveyed saw "nothing wrong" with sex before marriage. That percentage doubled (42%) by 1991. Forty-one percent of Americans condemned sex before marriage as "always wrong" in 1972. Only 27% held such a view in 1991 and I suspect the percentage is less today.

What is wrong? Simply this: men and women from all walks of life, from all ages and religious beliefs have moved away from the religious beliefs and the moral standards on which this country was founded. Many families are not willing to deal with the real issues facing them today.

More than 30 million people worldwide are now living with the HIV (AIDS) virus and some 16,000 victims are infected every day. One in every 100 sexually active adults worldwide is infected with HIV and only one in ten know that they are infected. If current transmission rates hold steady, by the year 2000 the number of people living with HIV/AIDS will be 40 million, a recent report said.

Frightening Statistics

The National Center of Health Statistics shows that there were 1,157,000 divorces in 1989 and in the first year of the 90's there was a total of 1,190,000 divorces. This statistical information was obtained directly from the divorce certificates that are collected by the Vital Records Office from each state and the District of Columbia. In 1990, 16.8 per 1,000 children under the age of 18 years were involved in divorce.

Why are divorce rates increasing? A study conducted at the University of Oklahoma shows that the no-fault law is what increased the divorce rate. The no-fault law caused already climbing divorce rates to jump further. Divorce rates in America zoomed to new heights under the no-fault law. In a study by Justec Research in Virginia on the effects of no-fault divorce in 38 states, the findings revealed "very strong evidence" that no-fault increased divorce in eight states and "some lesser evidence for increases in eight more." The study's author concludes that "on the average, no-fault laws increased divorces by some 20 to 25 percent." In none of the states studied did no-fault decrease divorce.

"No-fault" divorce laws are responsible for at least 20-25% of the increase in divorce rates.

What is the point? Couples today do not think they have to make their marriage last. It is just the way the world is today. God really does not care, so why make the effort. I believe that a very large number of divorcing couples do not even know or understand what God expects of a marriage. Do you?

Marriage Is for Life!

Ask yourself, "What is God's intention for my marriage?" God's intention for marriage is written in His Holy Word. Of course, not everyone is expected to marry but those who do fall in love and marry must know and understand what God expects from both partners—no exceptions. Each partner must understand what God, who made them from the beginning male and female, said in Matthew 19:4-6 as the Pharisees came testing Him and asking if it is lawful to divorce for any and every reason.

Successful marriage relationships require both partners to know (and to fully understand) what God expects from both the husband and wife....no exceptions!

"Haven't you read," He replied, *"that at the beginning the Creator made them male and female, and said, 'For this reason a man will leave his father and mother and be united to his wife, and the two will become one flesh'? So they are no longer two, but one. Therefore what God has joined together, let man not separate."*

What God says about all marriages and His will for marriage is very clear. The relationship of marriage is to be regarded as holy and must be given the highest priority by each marriage partner. What God has joined together should never be broken.

Can there then ever be grounds for divorce? Yes, but the grounds come from Holy Scripture and not on the basis of a general agreement of "It's not working—it would be best for us and the children to go our separate ways—we do not love each other anymore, we may as well go on and start over—we just are not compatible anymore—we have nothing in common—I would rather be alone than with you."

6

These are not reasons that God allows for divorce. We find the only reasons that God gives recorded in Matthew 5:31-32: *"It has been said, 'Anyone who divorces his wife must give her a certificate of divorce.' But I tell you that anyone who divorces his wife, except for marital unfaithfulness, causes her to become an adulteress, and anyone who marries the divorced woman commits adultery."*

The next portion of Holy Scripture that deals with divorce is recorded in Mark 10:2-9. Read it **READ MARK 10:2-9** carefully and think what it is really saying about divorce to you as an individual and a child of God. The Pharisees, testing Jesus, came and asked Him, *"Is it lawful for a man to divorce his wife?"*

"What did Moses command you?" He replied. They said, *"Moses permitted a man to write a certificate of divorce and send her away."*

"It was because your hearts were hard that Moses wrote you this law," Jesus replied. *"But at the beginning of creation God made them male and female. For this reason a man will leave his father and mother and be united to his wife, and the two will become one flesh. So they are no longer two, but one. Therefore what God has joined together, let man not separate."*

Holy Scripture further tells us in I Corinthians 7:10-16 where St. Paul writes, *"To the married I give this command (not I, but the Lord): A wife must not separate from her husband. But if she does, she must remain unmarried or else be reconciled to her husband. And a husband must not divorce his wife.*

Marriage Is for Life!

"To the rest I say this (I, not the Lord): If any brother has a wife who is not a believer and she is willing to live with him, he must not divorce her. And if a woman has a husband who is not a believer and he is willing to live with her, she must not divorce him. For the unbelieving husband has been sanctified through his wife, and the unbelieving wife has been sanctified through her believing husband. Otherwise your children would be unclean, but as it is, they are holy. But if the unbeliever leaves, let him do so. A believing man or woman is not bound in such circumstances; God has called us to live in peace. How do you know, wife, whether you will save your husband? Or, how do you know, husband, whether you will save your wife?"

In Hebrews 13:4 it tells us, "Marriage should be honored by all, and the marriage bed kept pure, for God will judge the adulterer and all the sexually immoral." A man or a woman who leaves the family for any reason and refuses to come back (desertion) is the only other reason allowed for dissolving a marriage.

Divorce is definitely not God's way of resolving marriage problems but our sinful natures leads us to ignore God's will for us. Our sin turns us AWAY from God but our sincere repentance turns us TOWARDS Him.

Divorce is definitely not God's way of resolving marriage problems. His standards do not change from one generation to another, but the sinful world and sinful people try to find ways to get around God's will. We saw it happen with Adam and Eve, and men and women still try to get away with not following God's will. Each man, each woman and each child suffers when this happens.

Why do problems arise in a marriage? Why do marriages fail? Because one spouse or both are not willing to give of self and take God at His Word. Both spouses must also understand what

8

sin and repentance means to each of them personally and to them as a married couple.

Sin and repentance need to be defined and understood in a world that has led many people away from their roots—HOLY SCRIPTURE. The Old Testament prophets conceived of sin as a personal and total aversion of man from his God and saw repentance as a personal and total turning to God. They deprecated any mere ritual repentance, *"Rend your heart and not your garments. Return to the Lord your God, for He is gracious and compassionate, slow to anger and abounding in love, and He relents from sending calamity" (Joel 2:13).*

The prophets demanded that man turn to God not merely ritually and formally but personally turn to Him in obedience and trust with a radical aversion from self and sin. *"Say to them, 'As surely as I live, declares the Sovereign Lord, I take no pleasure in the death of the wicked, but rather that they turn from their ways and live. Turn! Turn from your evil ways! Why will you die, O house of Israel?'" (Ezekiel 33:11).*

The prophets knew and more than once said that this turning is not a possibility with man but rests with God. *"Create in me a pure heart, O God, and renew a steadfast spirit within me" (Psalm 51:10). "I have surely heard Ephraim's moaning: 'You disciplined me like an unruly calf, and I have been disciplined. Restore me, and I will return, because you are the Lord my God'" (Jeremiah 31:18).*

John's call to repentance in the New Testament was universally as deep as it was wide. His appeal was more categorical even than that of the prophets. For it was made under the urging of the last days that only if a man and woman turn, really turn, can they be spared the judgment of God.

The President of The Lutheran Church— Missouri Synod, in urging his six thousand plus congregations to study the Word, has this to say. "Many refer to the age we live in as the post-Christian era. Today we are faced with a situation closely related to what the early church faced. Ethics and morality were relative, a philosophy of 'the end justifies the means.' When the early church was faced with this situation, it responded with a strong emphasis on teaching. It did not conform itself to the culture; instead it offered the alternative of an uncompromising faith in the one True God, revealed in the person of Jesus Christ."

A man or woman must have a right relationship and that means understanding who we are under God our Creator and where we stand as an individual. You must know that when you understand repentance and forgiveness, you can function as a whole human being in God's world. You can function as a whole because you know that Jesus Christ is your personal Savior. He died on the cross to pay the supreme price for all of your sins. God loves you, God loves your spouse and God loves your children.

God loves you, God loves your spouse and God loves your children.

So What Is the Point?

The point is, "Do we really believe what God's Word tells us about ourselves, about our spouse and about our marriage?" Psalm 10:14 says, *"But You, O God, do see trouble and grief; You consider it to take it in hand. The victim commits himself to You; You are the helper of the fatherless."* God wants husband, wife and children to be happy as He says, the two become one flesh. The husband is to love his wife as himself; the wife is to love her husband as herself. The point is, under no circumstances does God allow man and woman the option to dissolve their marriage. From the very beginning male and female were created to share life, to share God's fellowship and to have children, bringing them up in the nurture and admonition of the Lord.

When a marriage starts to break down, it is the responsibility of each partner to take whatever steps necessary to resolve the breakdown.

This means being willing to:

1. Pray
2. Grow in faith
3. Listen
4. Trust
5. Be honest
6. Be subject to God's will
7. Try to change with God's help
8. Be sincere
9. Be sympathetic
10. Be optimistic
11. Look at self
12. Be satisfied
13. Be tender
14. Be brave

When a marriage starts to break down, God is not a part of the marriage the way He should be. If the couple is going to get on the road to healing the marriage, each partner must be willing to read, study and listen to what God is saying to each of them.

This book is your personal manual. You need to make notes and write. So please use the extra margin space for your own notes, and use the couple's journal pages as indicated so that what you say becomes a part of you and your spouse. What you write you will be asked to share with your spouse as you grow back into a God-pleasing relationship.

Three Things to Remember

✻ We *do not have to accept* the cultural norms that contradict Biblical truths.

✻ With God's help, we *can* regain a right relationship with Him, our spouse and our family.

✻ God did not promise us that our lives would be easy and care-free, but <u>He did promise to be with us and to give us strength in times of trouble.</u>

Couple's Journal—For Her

What are your hopes and fears for your marriage?

Do you claim God's promise to help and sustain you?

Are you willing to study God's Word and apply it to your life and your relationship with your spouse?

....

....

....

....

....

....

....

....

....

....

....

....

....

....

Couple's Journal—For Him

What are your hopes and fears for your marriage?

Do you claim God's promise to help and sustain you?

Are you willing to study God's Word and apply it to your life and your relationship with your spouse?

....

....

....

....

....

....

....

....

....

....

....

....

....

....

❈ CHAPTER 2 ❈

Communication. . .

Communication. . .

Communication!

I am convinced that if married partners communicated together or if they will learn to communicate, their marriage can be on the path to a healing and lasting one as God intended it to be.

Webster's dictionary gives us these definitions of communication:

Communication and a willingness to learn the skills of communication are integral to getting and keeping your marriage on track.

1. To come to pass from one to another.
2. To transmit information, thought or feeling so that it is satisfactorily received.
3. To open into each other.
4. A verbal or written message.
5. A process by which information travels between individuals through a common system of symbols, signs or behavior. (Merriam Webster's Collegiate Dictionary, Tenth Edition)

What is communicated and what is received can mean life or death to the sender or receiver. Take the example of the luxury cruise ship the Titanic. A message was sent to the Titanic, "There are icebergs in the area." The builder of the ship said it was unsinkable, so the captain sped up in order to reach port a day earlier. The communication that took place caused horrible consequences for the ship's crew and its passengers.

Several years ago I was sent to Japan as an educational missionary, my family accompanying me. Wanting to make a good impression on the Japanese people, I tried to learn a few phrases in the Japanese language. One phrase I learned was "Where is the toilet?"—"Obenjo, doko desuka?" The other phrase that I learned was "Good morning!" "Ohayo gazimasu!" I learned the phrases by associating them with "banjo, the instrument" and "Ohio, the state." When I arrived in Japan with my family, intending to make a good impression on the first Japanese person I met, I blurted out "Iowa gazimasu!" I should have said "Ohayo gazimasu!" The poor Japanese gentleman looked at me like I was crazy and walked away. Communication is *knowing* what you are saying or writing and *meaning it* when you say or write it.

One failure was not enough for me. Some time later we were in a Japanese restaurant eating. I needed to go to the restroom and all of the signs in the restaurant were in Japanese. When the waiter came to our table to bring us water, I looked at the waiter and asked, "O banjo, doko desuka?" The waiter looked at me, smiled and left our table. Another waiter came bringing our food. I was still wanting to use the restroom, so I said to our new waiter, "O banjo, doko desuka?"

Communication, Communication, Communication!

He replied in broken English, "Just a minute, sir," and he left. After a few more minutes our first waiter returned smiling and carrying a large four-string banjo. Suddenly it dawned on me what the problem was—I had said BANJO rather than the word for toilet, which is BENJO!

I still needed to go to the restroom, which again stresses my point: COMMUNICATION, *COMMUNICATION*, **COMMUNICATION**! For any human relationship to be successful there must be proper and good communication.

Now for a marriage to be successful there must be communication between partners that is meaningful and allows the partners to feel good about themselves.

Communication between partners must be meaningful. It also must allow both partners to feel good about themselves.

One evening I was home with our exchange students from Japan. Marge was shopping. The doorbell rang and a good friend was standing at the door. Mary is 35 years old and her husband, Bob, is 38. It is the second marriage for both of them. Mary had big tears in her eyes and she was shaking. "I'm sorry, but I must see you. I have a big problem." I was shocked. I thought that something had happened to the family or Bob.

Her first words were, "I am getting a divorce, I just cannot take it any longer." I brought her into the living room, and the girls went upstairs to their rooms.

I said, "Mary, you are joking with me. You and Bob have a good marriage. What is wrong?"

"It may look good to you and other people," said Mary, "but not to me. I am just his work horse. All that we do is work seven days a week, go to bed, get up the next morning and repeat the same thing."

Mary went on, "We never talk or do anything. In my first marriage, I was abused and now this one is down the tubes. Al, what is wrong with me—is it my fault?"

"Mary," I asked, "does Bob know that you are here and telling me this?"

"No, we just cannot talk about anything and he just does not understand I am lonely. All he thinks about is making money. He does not love me anymore."

We talked some more. I asked her, "How long has this been going on, Mary?"

She replied, "A year or more. What made me come tonight is that he is going to spend the week with his mother at her cottage, and I have to stay with the business. Is that fair?"

She started to cry again. "You know that we are not active in church like we were. We have nothing in common anymore. I am afraid we have failed."

"Mary," I asked, "do you want this marriage to fail?"

"No, no but what can I do?" she asked. "He just clams up, walks out or goes to bed, and I am sick of it."

"Mary, may I talk to Bob and tell him you came to see me?"

She was silent for a couple of minutes and then said, "Yes, if he will come."

I told Mary that she had to tell him what she had told me. Mary left then and I continued my English as a Second Language class with the exchange students. The next day Bob called me and made an appointment. I told him that I wanted Mary to come, too.

He paused and then said, "O.K., if she will come. Al, I do not know what is going on, this is for the birds."

Bob and Mary arrived at my home the next evening. After a few pleasant exchanges, I went to the point of the visit. I asked, "Bob, what is the problem with you and Mary?"

Bob looked at Mary and then to me, "Al, I do not think we have a serious problem, but she sure does. We do not talk a lot, but you know me, Al, I do not talk a lot unless I am with the guys and have a beer or two. Mary and I have talked some since she came to see you. I guess we do have problems communicating. Maybe you can help us with this. I do not know why Mary is so uptight now."

Mary speaks up, "Bob, you do know what is wrong. You just leave me out of your life anymore, except when you want to use me. I feel like your whore. You use me and then make me run the business. Then you flip around up at your cottage with your mother and her friends and I am tired of it."

Now what do we have here? Two very fine people who it looks like are on the road to a broken marriage. I knew them well and had been involved with them socially, but I had no idea they were having problems and neither did their pastor or other friends and relatives.

What would Holy Scripture say to this husband and wife? I like the way Richard B. Hays puts it, *"Within the scriptural framework marriage is an analogy of God's faithfulness to His people. It is a binding commitment, not contingent upon the feelings of the partners."*

Marriage is an analogy of God's faithfulness to His people. It is a binding commitment, and is not contingent upon the feelings of the partners.

Marriage Is for Life!

These two people need to communicate together. For marriages to work the way God wants them to work there must be communication. From God, to the husband and the wife, and then as God's children there must be communication from one partner to the other partner, seeing each other as ONE in God's sight according to their marriage vows.

How does God communicate to the crown of His creation? In Holy Scripture, in Hebrews 1:1-2, He tells us, *"In the past God spoke to our forefathers through the prophets at many times and in various ways, but in these last days He has spoken to us by His Son."*

Again, in the Bible in Luke, Chapter 9, where Jesus was transfigured before Peter, James and John, it says, *"While Peter was speaking, a cloud appeared and enveloped them, and they were afraid as they entered the cloud. A voice came from the cloud, saying, ' This is My Son, whom I have chosen; listen to Him.'"*

If each partner, in faith, opens his or her heart to the communication of God, and applies that communication to the marriage, I can guarantee that the marriage will be on the road to recovery.

He also communicates in a very clear way how each couple can make it together as long as they live. What He says is simple and to the point. What happens is that many, many couples today fail really to accept what He communicates or misunderstand what He is communicating.

I can guarantee this, if each partner, in faith, opens his or her heart to His communication and applies it to their marriage, it will put their marriage on the road to recovery.

God communicates to a husband and wife through His Holy Word. He also expects the husband and wife to communicate to each other in Christ's love.

Communication, Communication, Communication!

Some couples have lived together since their wedding vows were said and have not communicated to each other. When I communicate with my spouse, as Webster has told us, there are many ways and levels of communication. "Marge, I am going to the store," or "I have to work late tonight," are simple daily conversations to keep a household running smoothly. This surface level of communication may still be functioning when a marriage is in trouble.

However, the real level of communication that should be functioning is not and that is the problem. I am talking about the level of communication that comes based on natural trust and respect for each other. If the level of trust is not there, Marge might respond to my going to the store in this way: "When will you be back? Are you stopping at the bar? Should the kids and I eat or will you be back for supper? You just got home from work, why do you have to leave now? What do you have to have that is so important?"

I might respond by slamming the door, getting into the car and roaring out of the driveway. The result? She is angry and I am angry and this is probably not the first time if the level of trust has been broken down through faulty communication or NO communication.

Let's follow the scenario a little further. After I speed out of the driveway, Marge may start to rationalize why I went to the store: "He did that just to spite me. . .He will be gone for hours. . .I work hard all day at home with the children. . .He did not even ask me how my day went!"

Her thoughts might continue to spiral downward until she is thinking, "I know he will stop at a bar and have a few drinks, more than he should. What is wrong with us, he just does not care about me any longer."

My feelings might go something like this, "What the heck is wrong with her? Anything I do she is always moaning and groaning: 'Stay home—don't go. You never play with the children. You drink too much.' All I was going to do today was go to the stupid hardware store and get some nails. I am ready to get out of this mess. All I do is work seven days a week and listen to a complaining woman who can't even keep the house clean."

What we have here is a marriage in trouble. Marge feels sorry for her real and imagined problems and sees her husband as unsympathetic and unloving. I feel sorry for myself because I see myself as being stuck with a nagging and suspicious wife. And I probably *will* stop at the bar for a drink.

The real problems are self-esteem, trust and proper communication. We will be dealing with trust and self-esteem later on. For now I want to continue with our concern about being able to communicate properly and in a way that the partners clearly understand what is being said.

The first step to healing must be a willingness to communicate with each other in a positive way.

There is no proper communication taking place when two partners have become angry or suspicious. For the healing process to begin the first step must be a willingness to communicate in a positive way.

Let's go back to the Marge and Al situation. On the way to the store let us say, for example, that something made me start to reflect back. "Could the problems we are having be my fault?" I make my purchase at the store, come directly home, walk into the kitchen where Marge and the kids are and say, "I am sorry. It was my fault for leaving like I did." Marge looks shocked and says that she is sorry too. This is where real communication could and should begin.

When I understand proper communication I can start on the road to reconciliation of my troubled marriage. I can *really communicate* with my partner when I am communicating with God in the proper way.

All matters must be right with God. He communicates to me and says that I am His child. In Jeremiah 1:5 He says, *"Before I formed you in the womb I knew you, before you were born I set you apart; I appointed you as a prophet to the nations."* What this tells us is that every person is a child of God and God has communicated His love to all of the people of the earth. He has set down a plan for each person and the Law which is written in each person's heart.

The Law tells us what to do and what not to do. The Law demands perfection but we are not able to be perfect because of our sinful nature.

God communicates to His children that because we cannot keep His laws He sent His Son, Jesus Christ, to keep what we are unable to keep for ourselves. Through Jesus, God enables us to be forgiven, and because I am forgiven, I can forgive my spouse.

Why then does a marriage get into trouble? Simply because one or both partners fail to listen to the communication that comes from God and when the partners fail to hear His communication, they fail to communicate with each other.

Because of our sinful nature, we are incapable of keeping God's Law. God sent Jesus to keep what we are unable to keep ourselves.

"We love, because God first loved us." Through Jesus, God enables us to be forgiven, and because we are forgiven, we too can forgive!

25

Seldom in today's society is this taught. We are often taught to make our own way, on our own. Janet put it this way. "I feel we should have been taught how to have a spiritual relationship with oneself long before we are let loose to procreate like animals and create a facade of normality when quite the opposite exists within our marriage."

Janet continues, "Often when a child is born, one parent more than the other expects everything to change the way they see fit. No discussion. The one spouse decides on child care—how, who and when will the child be cared for. Control issues seem to be a tremendous downfall at times. There is no compromising by communication in this situation because all of the decisions have been made."

Janet was divorced and has a sixteen-year-old son. She and Jack, her husband, both blame each other. You can still feel tension four years after the divorce. There is also a longing on both sides that the divorce could have been stopped. It is as if they both wish that someone would come up with a magic answer that would have made it all better.

Many divorced couples find that living apart is no magical solution. Especially when children are involved, they often feel as if they've traded one set of problems for another.

Janet said this: "I thought after we finally got a divorce things would be different. If I had it to do over again, I would have tried harder to have made it work, if for no other reason but for our son. After a divorce the child is left wondering, 'What is the family and where do I fit in? Did I cause Mom and Dad to break up?' A child is often left to pick up his or her own pieces."

Janet finished with these thoughts. "The reverence of two united seems to have been lost in our own self-centeredness, and children are left with broken hearts and many times blame themselves for something they had no control over. We can quickly see how lack of communication can hurt not only husband and wife but the children involved. It does not have to end in broken hearts.

"However, when there is lack of communication, as with us, the union breaks down. I believe if Jack and I could have communicated, we might have saved our marriage. I still have strong feelings about us and what we have lost forever. Our son is still paying the price. Surely God wanted more from our marriage than what has happened. Why?"

When there is lack of communication, the marital union breaks down.

I believe the answer to Janet's "why" is again lack of communication between her and Jack and their failure to understand or hear God's communication. Self-preserving and self-motivation can move each spouse away from the oneness in the marriage union with our love united in God and held in our souls to be one.

Self-preserving and self-motivation can move each spouse away from the oneness in the marriage union

When there is lack of communication, the union breaks down. The marriage breakdown can be reversed. How? By the partners recognizing that they can learn to communicate.

A friend recently said, "Many are taught how to divorce and the reasons for a divorce. Possibly one important point is to teach married couples in trouble the art of communication and how NOT to divorce."

To do this each partner has to be willing to try. Are you willing to try? If you are, your marriage can be saved. The willingness to try comes from each spouse understanding and accepting what

Are you willing to try?

God has communicated to His people and that is simply that divorce is unacceptable in His sight.

In His communication to every husband and every wife He puts it very clearly in Matthew 5:31-32. *"It has been said, 'Anyone who divorces his wife must give her a certificate of divorce.' But I tell you that anyone who divorces his wife, except for marital unfaithfulness, causes her to become an adulteress, and anyone who marries the divorced woman commits adultery."*

This is a difficult message for hurting couples to receive, that divorce is against God's Holy Will. But it is also a message of hope— God wants your marriage to succeed!

Jesus again communicates that the act of divorce is against God's Holy will. And so each spouse contemplates what this communication from the God-Man, Christ, means to each one of them.

Now that we have had a look at communication and the importance of being able to communicate honestly and sincerely, we know that real problems can be solved when honest communication takes place.

Holy Scripture communicates to us in Philippians 4:13, *"I can do everything through Him who gives me strength."* Christ is communicating to all of us that when we look to Him, when we trust Him, a failing marriage can be put back into a successful relationship. It is never "too late." NEVER say that it has gone too far.

I first met Rachel as I was participating in a "marriage in trouble" group. Rachel was married to Bob. She was 30 years of age and Bob was 34. I could see and feel the hostility in Rachel when the presenter explained that she had experienced what these couples are going through.

The presenter shared that she had been separated and on the verge of divorce and had said she could never be reconciled. Now in the first part of this presentation to Rachel, Bob and the others, the presenter explained that she and her spouse had indeed reconciled. Her partner and two teenage children are living together in peace and harmony, and her spouse was there before the group as living proof that no one should get a divorce.

The presenter asked the group to communicate, in writing, ten characteristics of their spouses. These are the ten characteristics that Rachel listed about Bob. Now remember, this is the first session—before the session on communication.

Characteristics of my husband:
1. *Bob has a mean disposition*
2. *Bob may not be trusted*
3. *Bob will lie and cheat*
4. *Bob cannot communicate*
5. *Bob hordes money*
6. *Bob's way is the only way*
7. *Bob walks on those around him*
8. *Bob loves himself*
9. *Bob tries to make me feel unworthy*
10. *Bob will never say "I am sorry"*

There was not one positive word about this person with whom she had vowed to be with as one. Remember your marriage vows, *"Will you have this man to be your husband, to live with him in Holy Marriage according to the Word of God? Will you love him, comfort him, honor him, obey him, and keep him in sickness and in health and forsaking all others, be wife to him as long as you both shall live?"*

Now we will turn to Bob and see what characteristics he wrote about Rachel.

Characteristics of my wife:
1. *Rachel is an airhead*
2. *Rachel is very self-centered*
3. *Rachel never uses any common sense*
4. *Rachel does not dress like she once did*
5. *It seems we have nothing in common*
6. *Rachel listens to her family too much*
7. *I do not trust Rachel with money*
8. *Rachel always wants to be on the go*
9. *She thinks the church can solve everything*
10. *She is too pushy with me*

Note the similarities in what these two partners have had to say about one another. Here we see partners in trouble.

In Ephesians 5:3 God's Word communicates some extremely important facts to each partner. *"But among you there must not be even a hint of sexual immorality, or of any kind of impurity, or of greed, because these are improper for God's holy people."*

Where do you stand regarding God's expectations for your behavior as a Christian?

When two spouses really believe that they are God's holy people, they begin to look at God's commands and see themselves and each other in a completely different light. And that is our goal, to help each partner take a look at what God is communicating and to make sure that each partner is communicating what is in the heart and from the heart as a child of God.

Let your communication come from the heart—as a child of God.

When each spouse takes God's communication to be what is expected and that there can be no exception, when the communication is clear and understood by each partner, they can accept God's communication as final.

Then a statement like the one made by a spouse after she and her mate had attended a marriage seminar, RETROUVAILLE (Retrovi) can be accepted as a fact that broken marriages can be healed and that more and more marriages are being saved.

What was her statement? "No matter what comes we are going to make it together." But let me say here that Retrouvaille is a real tool that can save a marriage in trouble, and it has put many back into a happy and functional setting.

What happened with Rachel and Bob after they read this chapter and attended the session on communication? These two, who had agreed not too long ago to a contract sealed by God "till death do us part," were asked to rewrite their communications about one another in a God-pleasing way.

Rachel was asked to make certain the characteristics she wrote were positive and that she agreed with them in this communication. Here is what she wrote:

31

Characteristics of my husband:

1. Bob loves his family
2. Bob is a good provider
3. I believe Bob is a Christian
4. Bob is friendly and people like to be around him
5. Bob is a hard worker
6. Bob knows how to get what he wants
7. The children respond to him in a positive way
8. He is fun to be with
9. He is very intelligent
10. He can make you laugh

In the above statements we see a real change in written communication about Rachel's spouse. Here we see the potential for healing to take place. In other words, if Bob can express himself in some positive ways about Rachel, there is hope.

We also know there is real hope for healing to take place when each spouse listens and takes to heart what God is communicating to them about their marriage.

Be willing to communicate with mutual respect for one another.

What each spouse must understand when a man and a woman desire to come together in the one flesh union of marriage is that communication is absolutely necessary for the marriage to be successful.

When two people living together as man and wife stop communicating, the entire family begins to fall apart. For a marriage to heal, the first step is a willingness to communicate with mutual respect for one another, and that is exactly what the Lord expects from His children.

Now that you have read the chapter on communication, turn to the journal pages and communicate your response to the questions you find there!

Three Things to Remember

* Divorce is against God's Holy Will. This is a sign of hope—for God wants your marriage to succeed.

* Effective communication is honest and open, but always shows a sincere, mutual respect for both speaker and listener.

* Take time to listen to what God is communicating to you through Scripture and allow the Holy Spirit to speak within you.

Three Things to Do

* Pray and ponder on the good things that have happened in your marriage.

* Write a letter to your spouse, sharing your feelings about the good things you see in your relationship.

* Complete the exercise in Chapter 2 by writing down ten characteristics of your spouse. Remember to communicate as a redeemed child of God. Share your list with your mate.

Couple's Journal–For Her

Define what communication means to you.

In what ways are you in communication with God?

What do I believe God's Word is communicating to my spouse?

What do I believe God's Word is communicating to my spouse and me about our marriage?

....
....
....
....
....
....
....
....
....
....
....
....
....
....
....
....
....

Couple's Journal—For Him

Define what communication means to you.

In what ways are you in communication with God?

What do I believe God's Word is communicating to my spouse?

What do I believe God's Word is communicating to my spouse and me about our marriage?

....

....

....

....

....

....

....

....

....

....

....

....

....

....

Chapter 3
God's Word, Will and Rule

When a marriage starts to break down I can tell you that there is a breakdown in the couple's relationship with God. In the book of Ephesians He tells us what we were and what we are after our relationship with Him is made right.

Do you know who you are and where you stand with God?

As a married couple in trouble, the first step to recovery is to know who you are and where you stand with God our Heavenly Father. As a couple and as individuals you must be willing to read, study and listen to what God is saying to you.

When we say we are Christian, but our marriage is not functioning, we have to ask, "Is this problem with me, with my partner or with my relationship with God?" We must remember that words literally provoke God to wrath when they are not more than talking the talk of repentance and faith. In Isaiah 5:20, God tells us through the prophet Isaiah, *"Woe to those who call evil good and good evil, who put darkness for light and light for darkness, who put bitter for sweet and sweet for bitter."*

Ask not according to what you "want and feel that we need to make our marriage work," but rather, "What would Jesus have me do? Lord, help me live my life according to Your will."

As each partner earnestly tries to deal with the marriage problem, the partner as a child of God must ask, "What would Jesus have me do as I live my life according to His will, not according to what I want and feel that I need and must have for my marriage to work?"

As you look at what the Bible has to say about marriage and the family that He expects to function in His world, we see just how far many of our cultural trends are from God's will for His children.

Married couples are exposed to signals with the wrong message which are contrary to God's Word in many movies, music, magazines, books and especially television. The message is sent that a sexual relationship outside marriage or before marriage is o.k.

Many in our culture today say that even a homosexual lifestyle is just an alternative to "traditional marriage." It is o.k. to do whatever is necessary to be "popular" among friends just as long as it feels good and you want to do it. If your marriage is causing you pain, get out of it and keep looking for the good life. These are just a few of the wrong messages today's society is throwing at us.

In the early church there was intense scrutiny of an individual who expressed an interest in becoming a Christian. A person's lifestyle was carefully examined. Before a person was accepted into a Christian community he had to demonstrate a sincere and genuine willingness to face any hardships that would come with being a Christian.

An early church leader, Hippolytus, demanded in his apostolic tradition that anyone who was involved in any form of immorality must immediately stop his or her sinful behavior. The convert had to choose between the worldly way or God's way as spelled out in God's Holy Word.

Do you as a Christian have any choice as you and your spouse see and know what God expects of you as a partner in your marriage? For better or for worse, in sickness and in health, in good times and bad times—divorce is not an option.

I say this to both partners; divorce is contrary to God's will. Jesus affirmed the divine institution of marriage during His earthly ministry in Matthew 19:5-6 where He said, *"For this reason a man will leave his father and mother and be united to his wife, and the two will become one flesh. So they are no longer two, but one. Therefore what God has joined together, let man not separate."* Here again in God's Holy Word there is absolutely no room for divorce.

The early church as it lived and responded to God's Word recognized that a convert to the faith was entering into a community of believers that was sharply distinguished from others in the way it viewed life. Marriage and accountability to God was expected as they lived their lives.

Early Christians faced the same pressures. Their lifestyle choices were sharply different from those around them.

Dr. William Weinrich is a well-known scholar and Academic Dean at Concordia Theological Seminary, one of two seminaries in The Lutheran Church—Missouri Synod. Dr. Weinrich said in an article on abortion and fellowship, "The freedom to choose has become privatized to personal opinion and preference. The claim that someone must behave in a particular way is regarded by post-modern culture simply as mean spirited, legalistic and oppressive."

The Lutheran Church—Missouri Synod is confessional and holds to the Bible as being without error. A document put out by The Lutheran Church—Missouri Synod's Commission on the Sanctity of Life says, "Life is given by God and is not for us to ignore according to our wishes."

It is the same with marriage which is instituted by God to bring precious life into the world. God's Word tells us that in the beginning God created man and woman to live with one another as husband and wife and through this union bring children into the world.

We read in Genesis 2:22-24, *"Then the Lord God made a woman from the rib He had taken out of the man, and He brought her to the man. The man said, 'This is now bone of my bones and flesh of my flesh; she shall be called woman, for she was taken out of man.' For this reason a man will leave his father and mother*

READ EPHESIANS 2:1-10.

and be united to his wife, and they will become one flesh."

Now I want each of you to look at Ephesians 2:1-10. I want to share with you what I believe it says to a hurting partner, and then what it says to other people who have endured pain and hurt in their married lives, but endured because they knew it was God's will and way for them.

What about you? In Ephesians 2:1-10 we read, *"As for you, you were dead in your transgressions and sins, in which you used to live when you followed the ways of this world and of the ruler of the kingdom of the air, the spirit who is now at work in those who are disobedient. All of us also lived among them at one time, gratifying the cravings of our sinful nature and following its desires and thoughts. Like the rest, we were by nature objects of wrath. But*

44

because of His great love for us, God, who is rich in mercy, made us alive with Christ even when we were dead in transgressions-it is by grace you have been saved. And God raised us up with Christ and seated us with Him in the heavenly realms in Christ Jesus, in order that in the coming ages He might show the incomparable riches of His grace, expressed in His kindness to us in Christ Jesus. For it is by grace you have been saved, through faith-and this not from yourselves, it is the gift of God-not by works, so that no one can boast. For we are God's workmanship, created in Christ Jesus to do good works, which God prepared in advance for us to do."

We are redeemed by God's grace, not by our own work or merits. It is not a decision we make but a gift that God gives.

The first part of the reading speaks to us telling us what we were before we belonged to Jesus Christ. Once we were dead, doomed forever because of our many sins. We used to live just like the rest of the world. **STOP**—How does the world live? Full of sin, obeying Satan, the mighty prince of power of the air. He is the spirit at work in the hearts of those who refuse to obey God.

The tempter wants us to fail in our relationships. Too often he succeeds, especially with those who are not grounded in the Word of God.

The world tells us to get out of a marriage—do what you want to do—it is too tough for you. The devil wants us to fail in relationships, and he succeeds with many people who really want to do what is right but are not grounded in the Word of God.

All of us used to live that way, following the passion and desires of our evil nature. We were born with an evil nature and we were under God's anger just like everyone else. This means that without God's will in a person's life it is easy to see failure in another person, it is easy to put another person down.

It becomes easy for spouses to feel that their partner does not measure up socially and the culture tells me if my partner does not measure up, then I can terminate the marriage.

It is never "too late," no marriage is "too far gone," because through God your marriage CAN BE HEALED, there is ALWAYS HOPE.

This is not God's way and your marriage does not have to be that way. God has a way that any marriage can be healed. No one can (nor should they) say there is no hope that their marriage cannot be healed, that it is too far gone.

Here again is why we must understand what it really means to be a child of God. Are you a child of God? Is your spouse a child of God? This is not a facetious question but a very serious question that you must answer. The answer dictates how you approach the healing of your marriage.

God says in the last part of the Ephesians passage that God is so rich in mercy and He loved us so very much that while we were dead because of our sins, He gave us life when He rose from the dead.

It is only by God's special favor that we have been saved. For He raised us from the dead along with Christ and we are seated with Him in the heavenly realms all because we are one with Christ Jesus. So God can always point to us as examples of the incredible wealth of His favor and kindness toward us as shown in all He has done for us through Christ Jesus.

God saved us by His special favor when we believed. We can't take credit for this, it is a gift from God. Salvation is not a reward for the good things that we have done so no one can boast about it.

For *we* are **God's** masterpiece. He has created us anew in Christ Jesus so that we can do good things He planned long ago for us. In God's Word He tells us, *"I can do all things in Him who has called us out of darkness into His marvelous light."*

What does this mean to you as a married partner? I believe it means simply that when we are God's children we are to look at our spouse through the eyes of Christ. We look at that person the way Christ looks at us.

When you look at your spouse, look through the eyes of Christ. Look at your mate as Christ looks at you.

Now when each spouse is willing to look at God's Word and say, "Where do I stand with my partner as a child of God because of what Christ did for me and my partner," healing CAN, WILL and MUST start to take place. The process may be long. It will take a commitment of both partners, but I can assure you it *will happen* when both partners stand under the will of God.

What is His will for your marriage? *What God has joined together **must stay** together.* When you took your vows you were joined together by God your Creator.

Now as we move toward the healing process and before you write what the Ephesians passage means to you, read what some other spouses have written about what it meant to them.

Marci wrote, "I am a sinner from the first, but I can and must ask for forgiveness. I must ask for me and for Jim. Maybe there is still a chance for us. These passages tell me that God is so merciful and that if Jim and I really repent, He will forgive us. Can I really believe this? I want to."

Marriage Is for Life!

My answer to Marci comes from Holy Scripture where we read in II Timothy 3:16-17, *"All Scripture is God-breathed and is useful for teaching, rebuking, correcting and training in righteousness, so that the man of God may be thoroughly equipped for every good work."*

Jim wrote after reading the Ephesians passage, "Regardless of our sins we are saved by God's grace. We should believe in God and His grace will be given to us. Can God help my marriage? It may be that Marci and I have not let God be in our marriage the way He should be. Reading this from God's Word makes me stop and think that we do need help."

Bill says, "This Scripture portion says that we are living a new life; this was given to us by Jesus when He died on the cross. A marriage must be lived by both parties. Where can you really get help when you feel like you need it? Who can you trust? You feel bad enough, as if you have failed and you do not want someone else seeing how you have failed. It hurts."

Peggy has this to say about what this reading means to her. "God's grace is a wonderful thing for me. He knows me and knows that I sin daily and that I fail daily, but He loves me just the same. He gave His Son to pay for all the wrong that I do. As His children, my husband and I must be subject to His will. So daily we must ask, 'What would God have us do according to His will?'"

Peggy makes a very valid point. A husband, a wife and a child of God must ask what it means when we say we believe in God and therefore are a child of God.

According to God's Word this is what it should mean: ***I hold and believe that I am a person who belongs to God, that He has given me my body, soul, life, mind, my reason, my understanding, wife, husband and children. He gives me all physical and temporal blessings. I cannot by myself preserve any of them. All of this is provided to me by my God.***

A great theologian has said, "If we believe what has been said here with our whole heart, we would act accordingly." This really is an important message for you and your spouse as you both work on healing your marriage.

Now that you have read how other couples have responded to the Ephesians portion of Holy Scripture, turn to your journal pages and consider your response to God's Word.

Remember that this book is your personal manual for you to make notes, so please use the journal pages and margin space as indicated so that what you say becomes a part of you and your spouse. You will need to share what you write with your spouse as you grow back into a God-pleasing relationship.

— STOP —
WRITE YOUR JOURNAL
RESPONSE NOW

Now that you have written down your thoughts re-read very carefully how you have responded. Is what you say in agreement with what God says? You know that it is His will that you and your spouse to resolve the difficulties in your marriage and live your lives as one in Him. God loves you. God loves your spouse. God loves your children.

God loves you. He loves your spouse and your children. God wants you to live a life in oneness in Him.

Thou Shalt Not Commit Adultery—This means that we should fear and love God that we may lead a chaste and decent life in thought, word and deed and each love and honor his spouse, a rule to consider when God joined a man and woman together to have children and enjoy life together as a family.

This lifelong union of one man and woman was instituted by God. God has therefore most richly blessed this estate above all others and in addition has supplied and endowed it with everything in the world in order that this blessed union may be provided for richly and adequately.

Married life is no matter to take lightly, but it is a glorious institution and one that is God's serious concern. It is of the highest importance to Him that families be brought up to serve God's world, to demonstrate what it means to be a child of God along with giving each man, woman and child eternal life through Jesus Christ.

In Holy Scripture where we receive the message of eternal life, He also provides for His children the Ten Commandments that tell us what we should and should not do. We also know that we cannot keep the Commandments.

However, as His children, He wants us to love and trust in Him and willingly do according to

His Commandments. In Matthew 22:36-40 Holy Scripture tells us that one of the experts in the law of that day tested Jesus with the following question, *"Teacher, which is the greatest commandment in the Law?" Jesus replied, "Love the Lord your God with all your heart and with all your soul and with all your mind. This is the first and the greatest commandment. And the second is like it: 'Love your neighbor as yourself.'"*

Luther says in the Large Catechism, "To each spouse this commandment requires everyone not only to live chastely in thought, word and deed in his or her particular situation (that is, especially in the estate of marriage) but also to love and cherish the wife or husband whom God has given." He goes on to say, "For marital chastity is above all things essential that husband and wife live together in love and harmony, cherishing each other wholeheartedly and with perfect fidelity."

We are called upon to love and cherish the wife or husband whom God has given.

When two people marry, God expects them to honor their pledge till death parts them. When a marriage fails to work out the way either spouse thinks it should, when blame starts to be leveled at your mate, it is time to stop and look within and ask the question, "God, where do I stand with You as I deal with this problem with my spouse?"

Having read this section about the Commandments, think about what it says to you as a child of God about your marriage. Take a look at how other couples responded:

After Brenda had read and thought about what this Scripture said about the Commandments, she had this to say, "I never really thought about

51

this Commandment. I studied it when I was in eighth grade in parochial school, but I have never really thought about it or thought how it fits into my life. John and I go to church most of the time. We have Brianne and I know that she senses something is not right with John and me. We try not to let her hear us argue. Most of the time we argue about money. We do not have as much as most of our friends and it hurts. I know we should spend more time in church and in God's Word. I just know if something or someone does not help us, we will not make it."

Now reader, what do you think the problem is here? I had Brenda read the material on the rule and then she shared some of her thoughts. Where should the focus on a marriage be? Certainly not on money or material things. I am not saying they are not important, but if the marriage relationship is right, money problems would not be pushing two partners and a little girl into trouble.

We say that we believe God our Heavenly Father not only has given us all that we have and see before our eyes, and He also, every day, guards and defends us against every evil and misfortune, keeping away from us all kinds of danger and disaster. If we believe what we say we believe, what does that say about a troubled marriage?

Simply this, that there is a breakdown between how you perceive your marriage and how God wants you as His child to treat your marriage. If God means what He says, He who has given you all, including your spouse, will guard and defend that relationship if we in Christian faith let Him.

God's Word, Will and Rule

Sad, but true, Ginna is 38 years old; her husband, Bill, was the pastor of a medium size church in the midwest. They had four children. Gina divorced Bill. She said, "Bill became so involved in taking care of the church that he neglected to take care of me and the children. I started to drink, Bill and I never communicated well, and it went from bad communication to NO communication at all. I blamed God and the church. Bill blamed me. We were sent to counseling, no choice of a counselor. I did not like the counselor and refused to go back. I saw no way out. I could not live up to being a pastor's wife. One night I just took the children to Bill's parents who lived nearby and left. We received a no-fault divorce. He has custody of the children. I guess you could still consider me a drunk and a failure. I am trying to get my life back together."

God, who has given you all, including your spouse, will guard and defend that relationship. Will you let Him do this work in you?

Gina and Bill are examples of a couple not getting help soon enough and not getting help that was acceptable to both partners. When either partner is not satisfied with the potential counselor, they must agree to continue to look until help is found that is agreeable to both parties.

The danger here is that an angry partner can jeopardize or stop the healing process by not being willing to use and follow through with the tools and help that God has made available for a marriage to start the healing process. Partners cannot look for roadblocks if they are going to get their marriage back on the road to recovery. The key is that both individuals recognize that God does not want a broken marriage and family.

You cannot look for roadblocks if you want your marriage to recover.

Both individuals must accept the fact that both have contributed to the problems in their marriage. It is easy to say, "Oh, yes, I know some of our problem is partly my fault." To really mean that and to be willing to work at solving the problems on the basis of God's Word, God's rule and God's solution means attacking the problems and being willing to resolve the problems, NO MATTER WHAT!

The "NO MATTER WHAT" is where the rubber meets the road. As a counselor, I have asked each partner, "Are you willing to really work at making your marriage work?" The answer in almost all cases from each partner has been "yes." However, the "yes" most of the time means "yes" on my terms and if my partner is willing to take all of the blame and willing to ask my forgiveness.

I want to talk about the Bible here again because if we understand its purpose and do not reject its purpose, the marriage can begin the healing process. The main purpose of the Bible is simply this: God gave the Bible so that the Holy Spirit can create saving faith in the reader, hearer and learner.

The Word of God is something alive and active. It cuts like any double-edged sword, but more finely it can slip through the place where the soul is divided from the spirit or joints from the marrow. It can judge the secret emotions and thoughts. Therefore, true believers hold the Bible sacred, respect its truths and submit to the teaching of the Bible.

What this means is that both partners submit to the Bible as the sole authority for their lives and the basis for any action that either partner takes as he and she take seriously what God tells them about His expectations of the marriage.

Three Things to Remember

❃ It is NEVER too late to save your marriage.

❃ We are saved and redeemed solely by God's grace. As children of God, we should endeavor to see our spouse through the eyes of Christ.

❃ God's will for marriage and marital fidelity is crystal clear. So also is His desire to help you preserve your marriage.

Three Things to Do

* Read Isaiah, chapter 5. Reflect on its meaning to you.

* Join an adult Bible study. Attend every week with your spouse.

* Find time EVERY DAY to read, learn and reflect upon God's word. Buy a cassette or CD version of the New Testament to play in the car.

Couple's Journal—For Her

Read Ephesians 2:1-10

What does this portion of Scripture say in general?

What does this portion of Scripture say to me as a child of God?

What does this portion of Scripture say about my marriage?

....

....

....

....

....

....

....

....

....

....

....

....

....

....

....

Couple's Journal—For Him

Read Ephesians 2:1-10

What does this portion of Scripture say in general?

What does this portion of Scripture say to me as a child of God?

What does this portion of Scripture say about my marriage?

....

....

....

....

....

....

....

....

....

....

....

....

....

....

....

....

....

....

CHAPTER 4

Accusation, Criticism and Blame

Accusation, criticism and blame must be dealt with if the healing process is going to take place between the two partners. It is good for us to go to Holy Scripture and see how Jesus Himself handled this situation.

In John 8:3-11 He tells us, *"The teachers of the law and the Pharisees brought in a woman caught in adultery. They made her stand before the group and said to Jesus, 'Teacher, this woman was caught in the act of adultery. In the law Moses commanded us to stone such women. Now what do you say?' They were using this question as a trap in order to have a basis for accusing Him. But Jesus bent down and started to write on the ground with His finger. When they kept on questioning Him, He straightened up and said to them, 'If any one of you is without sin, let him be the first to throw a stone at her.' Again He stooped down and wrote on the ground. At this, those who heard began to go away one at a time, the older ones first, until only Jesus was left, with the woman still standing there. Jesus straightened up and asked her, 'Woman, where are they? Has no one condemned you?' 'No one, sir,' she*

There is no place in a healing marriage for accusation, criticism or blame. Heed the word of the Lord, "Then neither do I condemn you," Jesus declared. "Go now and leave your life of sin."

*said. 'Then neither do I condemn you,' Jesus
declared. 'Go now and leave your life of sin.'"*

One of the most difficult things for a partner in
a hurting marriage is to keep from pointing the
finger at the other partner. As long as that accusing finger is being pointed, no progress can be
made.

As I grow older, I recall my grandfather telling
my cousins and me when we would tell on one
another that we were pointing one finger at
someone else and three fingers were pointing
back to us.

Listen to Sarah, "It has never been the same
since the children were born. It started when I
was pregnant with Susie. When I started to lose
my figure, Ken started to lose interest. It was his
fault that I was losing my figure. When I was big
he did not want to go places with me. I know he
started to look at other women and that had
really hurt me. When I was pregnant with Ken,
Jr., it was worse. I don't think either of us wanted
our second child at the time."

Here is how Ken perceives the situation. "When
Sarah became pregnant with our first child, you
would not believe how she changed. She accused
me of not caring about her now that she was pregnant. She accused me of flirting with other
women when we went out. These accusations
made me angry and I started to do things that I
knew would upset her. Then she would go crying
to her mom and dad, who had spoiled her and her
sister, and this made me more angry. When she
was pregnant with Ken, Jr., it was worse than
with Susie. Sarah accused me of really wanting

her to have an abortion. That is not true but she believed it anyway."

Ken further states, "We argue and fuss a lot and always accuse each other for what goes wrong. We went to see our pastor a few times and we started blaming each other in front of him. That was embarrassing for me. I would not go back to counseling again. I did not like to go to church—when the pastor greeted us at the door, he seemed to be embarrassed. What does the church have to do with our problems anyway? I think Sarah and I just may not be suited for one another. Is it worth it? I do not know any more. I do know I love my children."

It is easier to blame others than to admit, "It is my fault."

We can see that both Sarah and Ken are hurting, and we know that it is not easy to say, "I am to blame." Our sinful human nature wants to place all of the blame for the problems in the marriage, not on ourselves but on our spouse. Even when some other person tries to help, they may be blamed.

In the beginning Ken wanted to blame their pastor for poor counseling. I had the opportunity to talk together with Ken and the pastor after Ken decided that in order to save the marriage he and Sarah would have to work through their problems and that their pastor was a vital link in the recovery process for their marriage.

Your pastor is a valuable advocate in healing your marriage. Like Ken and Sharon's pastor, he can help you to look beyond selfish needs and focus on a real partnership based on your vows.

Ken and Sarah, because of their love for their children, made a commitment to each other that they would do whatever was necessary to make their marriage work. Ken explained to me, in front of his pastor, that his pastor had really been the one to help him and Sarah look past their selfish needs. These two people, with the leadership of their pastor, started the slow process of re-establishing a marriage partnership based on the vows they made on their wedding day. I say slow because their pastor had helped them to see that the relationship will not be mended in a week or two but a lifetime of taking one day at a time.

Each partner must be willing to take not just some of the blame for marital problems; each partner must be willing to assume ALL OF THE BLAME.

Each partner in the relationship must overcome the finger pointing and blaming the other partner for all the problems in the marriage. Each partner must also be willing to do some sincere soul searching and ask the question, "What can I do each day to let my partner see that I am willing to take the blame, not just part of the blame but all of the blame?"

Chances are the reader is starting to react and think, "We are both to blame." I tell the reader, "If healing is going to take place, you need to say to yourself, 'I am the only one to blame and I need to look within to see my problems and ask the Lord to take my pain away so that I can begin to participate in the healing process of our marriage.'"

Perhaps a story can most clearly illustrate this point. It was on a Thursday morning, about 11:30, and I needed to get home for lunch so that I would get to my 12:30 class. Dan burst into my office and said, "I must talk to you. I have a divorce. Now I need to decide whether I can stay in the ministry. I value your advice. Tell me what you think I should do."

Eighteen years ago I had taught this pastor on a college campus and was acquainted with his lovely wife. Now out of the blue he pops into my office and tells me his marriage is broken up and his children are with their mother.

Here is the interesting point for us. The conversation from him continued like this, "The divorce is all my fault. I am absolutely to blame."

This is his explanation of why he is to blame. "I enjoyed my congregation and all the challenges it presented to me. I worked long hours making calls, counseling and doing all the things I think a good pastor should do while Paula and I just drifted apart. I would come home after a day at the office, eat dinner and return to the office for meetings or other responsibilities. On Sunday after services I would take a nap while watching TV and go to bed early in the evening.

"Our parish loved us both and thought we were the ideal role model for the church. They had no idea what I was putting Paula through. She told me I was married to the congregation and she was my maid. I really abused her and our two children ages 6 and 13. The divorce came because Paula finally had an affair. I believe she had this affair so I could get a divorce and be allowed to stay in the ministry.

"Paula has gone through some difficult times since our divorce was finalized six months ago. Things have gone well with me. The congregation has been very supportive. My bishop has been very supportive and is willing for me to stay in the ministry but what do you think?"

I told Dan, "It is not what I think, but what does God say?"

God tells Dan that marriage is the lifelong union of one man and one woman into one flesh. This union between Dan and Paula was instituted by God.

Marriage Is for Life!

Matthew 19:6 says, *"So they are no longer two, but one. Therefore what God has joined together, let man not separate."* Holy Scripture in Ephesians 5:24-25 says to Dan and to every person reading this book, *"Now as the church submits to Christ, so also wives should submit to their husbands in everything. Husbands, love your wives, just as Christ loved the church and gave Himself up for her."*

To the point in his life when Dan and Paula divorced, they both had let Satan use their marriage to feed their selfish needs. Paula used another individual and Dan used the congregation. They both used their children as pawns to find fault with one another and used the church as an excuse to hide their problems from each other and people who could have helped.

Dan finally realized the problem when he lost Paula and the children. He knew he was wrong and that he had done an injustice to Paula, the children and the congregation. His words, "It was all my fault," I believe, are a real acknowledgement of sin. He is not playing games. He knows what he must now do according to what God's Word tells him to do.

It is really never "too late." Even after a divorce becomes final, reconciliation can take place.

This is what Dan did on the basis of what Holy Scripture had to say to him. He went to Paula and told her that he had sinned against her and their children, that all of the problems that led up to her infidelity and their divorce were his fault, that he had abused her and the children by not giving them time and attention. He told Paula that he was sorry and wanted her forgiveness. He said that because of the marriage vows they had made before God he wanted them to reconcile, for

Paula's sake, for his own sake and for the sake of their children.

What made Dan change his attitude toward himself, Paula and the children, toward his responsibility, and toward his marriage vows? The change was brought about by what Holy Scripture said to him when he finally took the time to ask himself the following questions:

1. Do I really believe what God tells me?
   (His answer was "YES!")
2. Will God heal my marriage?
   (His answer was "YES!")
3. Do I love my children?
   (His answer was, of course, "YES!")
4. Can I forgive?
   (His answer was "YES!")
5. Do I need to be forgiven?
   (His answer was "YES!")
6. Can I live with my wife?
   (His answer was "YES!")

This couple came to the realization that there was blame on both sides. When each of them had to answer the question, "Do I really believe what God tells me?" their approach to the possibility of healing their marriage took on new meaning and a real desire on their part to keep the vows they made on their wedding day.

You see when accusation, criticism and blame can be placed at the foot of the cross and when the couple really believes what God tells them, healing can take place. That is the beauty of the Gospel.

Believe in God's promises, and lay the accusation, criticism and blame at the foot of the cross. God's healing hand can help you. This is the beauty of the Gospel of our Lord Jesus Christ.

Marriage Is for Life!

There is a song that says, "His blood can make the vilest sinner clean." Holy Scripture tells us in I John 1:7, *"But if we walk in the light, as He is in the light, we have fellowship with one another, and the blood of Jesus, His Son, purifies us from all sin."* That is the way God commits Himself to His people. He said, *"I will be your God. Whatever happens I will never leave you."* That is how God wants the husband and wife to understand their marriage relationship and their relationship with God.

Not long ago I was in my doctor's office early in the morning. A lady sat down next to me. After saying good morning she was looking in her wallet and dropped it on the floor. Photos fell out of the wallet beneath my chair. I picked them up and handed them to her. One photo was of a young girl. I commented on the beauty of the young lady in the picture. The woman smiled and responded that the photo was her daughter.

We started a conversation about teenagers. I told her that I was working on this book and that one of the chapters deals with children of divorced parents and what research has to say. It simply shows that it is better for the children to be with both parents even if the marriage has rough edges and mother and father fuss a lot.

The lady then told me that she was divorced and how hard it had been for her daughter. She now believes that couples should stay together for the sake of the children unless there is physical abuse. There is research to support how this woman feels.

This mother told me the most significant factors in her divorce started out as little disagreements.

Accusation, Criticism and Blame

Each one blamed the other for not spending money wisely when there were more bills than money. She said she felt their marriage came to an end because of the criticism and blame over money problems and the disagreement on how to discipline their daughter.

Then with tears in her eyes she said, "I must say that although my husband and I were raised by Christian parents, always went to church, neither of us had an active faith. Oh, we believed there is a God but He was not a real part of our married life."

She told me she had learned what Jesus Christ really means since her divorce. Knowing Him and laying all of her hurt and blame on Him has enabled her to have a satisfying life with her daughter. She misses being married and feels a sense of loss that will never really go away. She said if she had it all to do over again, she would not give up so easily. Living a single parent life is not easy for the adult or the child.

Use the journal pages to work through your thoughts and feelings about accusation, criticism and blame. Look back at the questions Dan asked himself. Are you able to echo his fervent "Yes!"?

Remember, you are not in this alone—as a young wife in a recent seminary pointed out, with a strong faith in Jesus Christ every couple can overcome the day-by-day challenges that can lead to serious marriage problems with our Lord being a part of that marriage. Romans 10:17 tells us how that faith grows, *"Consequently, faith comes from hearing the message, and the message is heard through the Word of Christ."*

Three Things to Remember

❊ Your pastor is a valuable advocate and mentor as you work together towards a healthy marriage.

❊ Each partner must be able to admit, "I am the only one to blame."

❊ Believe in God's promise. Take your hurt, anger, guilt and blame to Christ. The Grace of the Gospel can bring you peace.

Three Things to Do

* Write down all of your anger, hurt and frustration. Seal it in an envelope. Give your anger and hurt over to the healing of Christ. Shred or burn the envelope and its contents as a symbolic reminder of your resolve to keep accusation, criticism and blame out of your relationship.

* Get something for your spouse that will remind them of Christ's love. Include a card or flowers and a note expressing your willingness to see them through Christ's eyes.

* Go to church with your spouse and family. Get involved in family activities at church. Set aside a time for family devotions.

Couple's Journal—For Her

What does the Bible say to you about each of the following:
Accusation: Criticism: Blame:

What needs to happen to help a marriage heal?

Do you really believe what God says? Why?

What does He say about faith in Him?

How does God want to heal a marriage?

....

....

....

....

....

....

....

....

....

....

....

....

....

Couple's Journal–For Him

What does the Bible say to you about each of the following:

Accusation: Criticism: Blame:

What needs to happen to help a marriage heal?

Do you really believe what God says? Why?

What does He say about faith in Him?

How does God want to heal a marriage?

....
....
....
....
....
....
....
....
....
....
....
....
....
....

❃ Chapter 5 ❃

Children in a Troubled Marriage

The most heartbreaking result of a marriage that is breaking up is what happens to the children. Every divorced mother and father that I have ever talked to about the effect divorce has had on their children always responded in much the same way, "If I had known how much my children would suffer, and still do, I would have tried much harder to make the marriage work, just for the sake of my children."

Every parent worries about the effects of divorce on their children.

As you read this chapter, if you and your partner are still considering the possibility of divorce, let me point to some problems that our youth face today. Many of the challenges they face come from a marriage that has failed or one that is failing.

Your marriage is worth preserving, even if only for the best interests of your children.

This is a true story that eighteen-year-old Bill related to his pastor. Everyone predicted that Bill would be highly successful. He was an only child. He was a star athlete as a freshman in his high school and his grades were very good.

One morning Bill stopped in the pastor's office and informed him that his mother and father were getting a divorce. He couldn't believe it and felt it must be his fault. He wondered, "What have I done?"

His parents told him they would let him decide with whom he wanted to live. His response was that he could not make that decision because he loved both of them very much. "What can I do? Help me, Pastor, tell me what to do."

Our new trend of affluence, and rebellion from our biblically based moral values, leads to the breakdown of the home and has permitted parents to be free to walk away and leave the schools and society to take care of their children. Here are some of the things that are happening to these hurting young people today.

Statistics for troubled teens are staggering. The consequences to our children are tragic.

Every 60 minutes 58 children attempt suicide, 114 run away from home, 28 teenage girls give birth to illegitimate babies, 180 receive a "legal abortion."

The most precious gift God gives to a husband and wife are children, and parents are hurting children in so many ways that it is high time they put their child or children first; not so far as material things but time, stability and love... love... love. This means that you stay in a marriage and make it work if for no other reason than for your children.

A group of prominent educators recently pointed out that increased demands made by families have forced schools to act as parents in many cases, and it is especially true when spouses are having marital problems.

A noted author recently told a parent group that "Parents cannot leave the responsibility of raising their children to the schools and society." We expect them to grow up as normal productive adults but with little family structure. Many times both parents are dysfunctional regarding parenting.

What's wrong? One recent survey shows that 30% of babies are born to unwed mothers and 25% of children live with one parent. ***Children need both parents.***

Another survey study challenging single motherhood found that fathers are especially important to girls for self-esteem and success. Still society continues to promote the idea that it is perfectly alright and morally acceptable to be an unwed mother.

Fathers are especially important to girls for self-esteem and success. Teen-age promiscuity and pregnancy are dramatically higher for girls without a father in the home.

Kathleen Parker, in an article entitled "Scarcity of Dad a Tragedy," goes on to say that even without research, we have observed in recent years an increase in youth violence, teen pregnancy, drug abuse and the absence of a father—is there a correlation? I believe there is a high correlation and a reason why more must be done to help married couples stay together, again, if for no other reason than for the children brought into the world by their marriage before God.

Now we realize that God loves each man, woman and child so much that He sent Jesus, His Son, the God-man to give life to all who listen to Him. What does this God-man, Christ Jesus, who gave His life for you and your spouse have to say about divorce? Listen again to the words found in Mark 10:2-12, *"Some Pharisees came and tested Him by asking, 'Is it lawful for a man to divorce his wife?' 'What did Moses command you?' He replied. They said, 'Moses permitted a man to write a certificate of divorce and send her away.' 'It was because your hearts were hard that Moses wrote you this law,' Jesus replied. 'But at the beginning of creation God "made them male and female." For this reason a man will leave his father and mother and be united to his wife, and the two will become one flesh. So they are no longer two, but one. Therefore, what God has joined together, let man not separate.' When they were in the house again, the disciples asked Jesus about this. He answered, 'Anyone who divorces his wife and marries another woman commits adultery against her. And if she divorces her husband and marries another man, she commits adultery."*

God tells us that marriage is a lifelong union of one man and one woman into one flesh.

This is very clear for the husband and wife. God is telling His people that marriage is the lifelong union of one man and one woman into one flesh. He says in a very simple and clear way that when two people marry, He expects them to stay married as long as they live. Why? Because of that precious gift, **CHILDREN!** In every man and woman there is a natural desire to bring life into the world, and God tells us how He wants us to raise them.

He tells us to, *"Train a child in the way he should go, and when he is old he will not turn from it"* (Proverbs 22:6).

The work of the Holy Spirit that makes disciples of people begins with baptism, and continues with prayer, Bible study and Christian precepts taught by both parents and nurtured by the church.

Many sociologists and researchers tell us the family is dying. Possibly we should think of our families like the Canadian road sign I saw, "Be careful which rut you fall in, you may be driving in it for the next 25 miles."

Is divorce really worth it? Ask your son or daughter.

Each spouse in a marriage must ask whether or not the divorce they are contemplating is worth the risk they are bringing to their children.

The goal for your child should be that of a growing and happy individual with the ability to love, work and play in the home and community where God has placed him or her. For this to happen the child must have parents who have their priorities and view of family in the proper perspective.

What this means is simply that children must be in an environment created by moms and dads, the church and school where they can develop a self-esteem and a feeling of worth and confidence that enables them to reach their God-given ability. The closer we as parents are to God's plan, the more successful we are in helping our children feel secure and happy in the family structure.

The closer we, as parents, are able to remain to God's plan for us and our families, the more successful we will be in helping our children feel secure and happy.

II Timothy 3:14-15 makes very clear the role of both parents as they bring their children up in the nurture and admonition of the Lord. We are told, *"But as for you, continue in what you have learned and have become convinced of, because you know those from whom you learned it, and how from infancy you have known the Holy Scriptures, which are able to make you wise for salvation through faith in Christ Jesus."*

In I Peter 2:9 we read where God wants you as a family, joined by marriage till death do you part, to know exactly who you and your children are.

He tells us, *"But you are a chosen people, a royal priesthood, a holy nation, a people belonging to God, that you may declare the praises of Him who called you out of darkness into His wonderful light."* Now look at what He tells husbands and wives in verse 12. *"Live such good lives among the pagans that, though they accuse you of doing wrong, they may see your good deeds and glorify God on the day He visits us."*

Parents must be willing to sacrifice their needs for the needs of their children.

Every child that is denied both parents because of a divorce is cheated, and both parents must be willing to sacrifice their needs for the needs of the children that the two of them have brought into this world. As parents we must recognize that love is the key. Love says you are forgiven as my partner and as my spouse.

God's love in action through our Savior's death on the cross enables parents to see as Christ's redeemed. We are His role models, called to be examples, called to give guidance, direction and discipline to our children who want and NEED it.

"God has not given you your children and the means to support them simply so that you may do with them as you please or train them for you just to get ahead in the world. They belong to God."

If one parent fails to know or do his or her part in the role of the support system, then all of the family will begin to suffer. A great educator and preacher made this point: "God has not given you your children and the means to support them simply so that you may do with them as you please or train them for you just to get ahead in the world. They belong to God."

The point I want to make is simple. If both spouses see the needs of their children as God sees their needs, divorce becomes out of the question and the parent in each case must then ask how he or she can provide the home environment needed for their children to develop into well-rounded Christian adults able to live as God's children.

When we see the kinds of problems that are occurring in our schools today, I can assure you as a former teacher, principal and superintendent that the major cause of children's problems in school stem from problems in the homes.

Most behavioral and academic problems at school are a result of problems in the home.

One of the problems is that mom and dad are so caught up in work and social life that they feel guilty. The child in turn is provided everything he or she desires but denied the one thing they need most, the proper amount of quality time and tough love that enables the parents to know what is going on with friends and at school.

This means daily interaction between parent and child. A parent must be prepared to say with great meaning, "Yes, you will" or "No, you will not" and stand behind it. When a child is putting himself or herself at risk and the parents know it, we, in general, are failing to help our children really understand what the role of a parent is in their lives.

First and foremost, children need to know and believe that they are a blessed gift from God to their parents. They need to know and be told that they are wanted and loved by their mother and father. They need to know that as they grow each day there are boundaries set in the home and expectations laid down by the school and supported by the parent.

The parents and schools must work together to provide a secure environment for their children. It is a fact that most children who have problems in school and dealing with their peers come from a home that has a mom and dad whose priorities are mixed up or a single parent struggling to survive in an economic, social and parenting squeeze.

What is the point? If mom and dad, son and daughter are going to have a normal life as God wants them to, the parents have the awesome responsibility of bringing children up in the nurture and admonition of the Lord.

"You show me a family that is in God's Word every day, and I will show you a family that will make it in His world as His family."

For parents to know their responsibilities they must understand the Law and Gospel and apply it. A senior pastor friend put it like this, "You show me a family that is in God's Word every day, and I will show you a family that will make it in His world as His family."

What makes the difference? Spouses who know what God expects of them, and that means from conception that they as parents bring this gift of life to God's house for worship.

The child attends Sunday School while parents attend Bible Class and then, as a family, worship together in church. This means **every** Sunday, not just when it is convenient.

What I want you to understand, as husband and wife and as parents, is that when you see your spouse and your children the way God does, and because of what He sent His only begotten Son to do for us in that while we were still sinners, failures and nobodies, He made us and our children His children with the guarantee of life forever in paradise.

John 3:16 tells us, *"For God so loved the world that He gave His one and only Son, that whoever believes in Him shall not perish but have eternal life."*

Children in a Troubled Marriage

When you, as a husband and wife stand before their Maker as His children, you cannot look to divorce as a way to solve the problems you are having in marriage.

You can look to Him for guidance and direction. We see a sinful world and recognize there is no permanence in this world without faith and trust in Jesus Christ. With faith comes a guarantee of permanence, a solution to the problems in your marriage, a way to bring the kind of love and care that is necessary for a child to grow up which comes from a mother and father who see in their marriage the absolute responsibility of raising their children to adulthood in a firm, fair and reasonable environment, that puts the child ahead of the needs of each other if that kind of decision needs to be made.

Look to God for guidance and direction as you navigate the turbulence of the world.

What is important for you as parents is that *your child needs both of you—mother and father.* Even if that is the only reason you can find to make your marriage vows work in the proper way—to do what is right for the life that the two of you brought into the world as a precious gift from God, He will give you the guidance and direction to do so if you will ask Him and mean it.

Use the journal pages and questions to guide you as you examine your thoughts and feelings about parenting.

Three Things to Remember

❋ God's vision for a family includes two parents. Your children need to know you will not abandon each other or them.

❋ Children are a precious gift from God and are entrusted to their parents' care and nurture.

❋ Your child's best chance at a happy and successful life lies in a nurturing Christian home where he knows he is loved and wanted.

Three Things to Do

* ❋ Write a note (or make a tape recording or video) telling each of your children how special they are in God's eyes (and yours) and just how much you love and care about them.

* ❋ Eat dinner together every night. Begin or end the meal with a devotional time suited to the age of your children

* ❋ Make a "kid sandwich" by hugging your spouse with your child in the middle.

Couple's Journal–For Her

Define a responsible parent.

What does God expect from you as a parent?

What can I do to save my family from divorce?

What is the danger for children from single-parent homes?

....

....

....

....

....

....

....

....

....

....

....

....

....

....

....

Couple's Journal—For Him

Define a responsible parent.

What does God expect from you as a parent?

What can I do to save my family from divorce?

What is the danger for children from single-parent homes?

....

....

....

....

....

....

....

....

....

....

....

....

....

....

....

❉ Chapter 6 ❉
A New Beginning

E very divorced person I have ever talked
with has at some time during the conversation said they wish they could have a
new beginning. If only they could have a new
start, if only they knew when they got the divorce
what they know now, they would have tried
harder to make it work.

No matter which former partner I have spoken
with, it is always the same; if only I had known
how bad the hurt would be and still is, I would
have tried some way for a new beginning. This
book points the reader in that direction. There
can be a new beginning if both parties are willing
to let God's Word direct their marriage into new
beginnings.

There can be a new beginning if both parties are willing to let God's Word direct their marriage into new beginnings.

How? Sarah related her and Alan's new beginnings in the following way: "Our marriage hit
bottom after two years. Our problems began
when we found out I was pregnant six months
into our first year of marriage. We had laid out a
five-year plan with both of us working at good
jobs. We bought a new car, purchased a home and
a child was not in the picture.

"To make a long story short, our marriage went
down hill from the day I told Alan I was pregnant.

Marriage Is for Life!

Sarah, a young mom whose married life hit rock bottom when she became pregnant, says, "to anyone thinking about a divorce, it does not have to be."

Both of us had good loving parents and they were devastated when I moved back into their home when our baby boy, Alan, Jr., was three months old.

"I was heartbroken, depressed, worthless and mad at God and my world was out of control. But let me say here to anyone thinking about a divorce, it does not have to be.

"There can be a new beginning. Ours started slow. When we separated we decided that it would be a friendly divorce as the lawyer we talked with expressed it. I would keep the baby. Alan would pay support of $2000 per month and we would sell the equity in our house, what little there was. We just needed to get out of the mortgage.

"Then our pastor asked us to wait six months before we would sign the papers. Parents and friends on both sides of the family gave us mixed signals and advice. Going to church really had not been a high priority for us. I knew this was wrong and so did Alan, but we had been too busy. But now reality of what was happening hit us both. We needed help and pastor was trying to help. He knew that Alan and I first needed spiritual help if our marriage could be salvaged.

"Alan and I knew it, too but we were resentful and stubborn. Pastor said it was up to us and he would like to suggest something for us to consider, but the choice was ours. However, it was important and vital for us to make sure as God's children that we do what is right in His sight.

"Pastor said, 'It must be God's decision on how we live our lives.' He pointed out that we must not make decisions based on our needs and feelings

100

that are contrary to what God desires and demands. We agreed to meet with pastor.

"As we met with pastor he shared how we might save our marriage and make a new beginning. Both Alan and I realized that when we said our vows before God on our wedding day, we had made a commitment forever as long as we both have life.

"Now, even though we had not planned for a baby to come along when it did, we made the baby. Alan, Jr. belonged to God and we were the caretakers. I love my baby and I want the best for him. I believe Alan loves him and wants him to grow up in a good home environment.

You can find a new beginning in your marriage. The road is not always easy, and there will be challenges to overcome. But, like Sara and Alan, with God's help you can make it work, one day at a time.

"What could two hurting people do? We would have preferred to just run away from the entire situation—just make it go away. Alan and I found out that running away is not real life. We found help and we were able to make a new beginning in our marriage. It was not an easy road to follow and there have been challenges every day, but we are making it one day at a time."

How could this young couple save their marriage? The first step for them was being willing to say that the marriage should be saved and both were willing to try. The answer to why it should be saved was simply that they were willing to sit down with their pastor and be led through Holy Scripture. The reader has already been exposed in this book as to what God's Word says. Sarah and Alan's pastor pointed out very clearly how important it was for them to know that the Lord knows our weaknesses and our strengths. He knows our intentions and our transgressions.

Our Lord tells us in Jeremiah 16:17, "*My eyes are on all their ways; they are not hidden from Me, nor is their sin concealed from My eyes,*" and in Luke16:15 we are told, "*You are the ones who justify yourselves in the eyes of men, but God knows your hearts.*"

The point for Sarah and Alan and all who really want to save what God joined together on that day when wedding vows were spoken is that the relationship with God must be "right," and "right" means that Sarah and Alan and all others know that they and their children are His and that He is theirs.

The pastor also pointed out what a great preacher and counselor had to say about faith and love. He rightly stated that, "Faith receives and love gives." Faith brings one to God, and each spouse must be able to live that faith in action toward spouse and children. Love brings reconciliation to wife, husband and child. Then new beginnings have a base on which to start a new marriage relationship that can have real and lasting relationships. This means I show care and concern for my spouse and my child, because I see these people as gifts from God to me and for whom I am responsible and accountable to God.

We are able to see several very important reasons that Sarah and Alan are making a change in their marriage from separation and divorce to being back together in a marriage becoming stronger each day.

The first step toward reconciliation is that Sarah and Alan were willing to recognize that they had stopped communicating with one another. Through their pastor they were able to

"Faith receives and love gives." Faith brings one to God, and each spouse must be able to live that faith in action toward spouse and children. Love brings reconciliation to wife, husband and child.

see that their failure to communicate had driven them farther and farther apart until the separation took place. As they started to communicate they listened to what each other had to say. This is not an easy thing to do. It takes a great deal of self-control and also means that I am to keep my mouth closed and listen to what my spouse is really saying.

You might read the chapter on "Communication" one more time at this point. When real communication can take place with God and His two children (the husband and wife), new beginnings are off to a positive start.

Read Chapter 2: **Communication, Communication, Communication!** *again to see how much you've learned.*

A simple way to begin is for you to ask your spouse to pray with you. This step comes after you have looked inside your innermost being and after you have communicated with your Heavenly Father, and when you have been able to quit blaming and are willing to let the Lord work in both of you to will and to do of His own good pleasure.

In Holy Scripture He tells us to pray to Him. He tells us to ask and He will always answer. Now the important point to remember is the fact that He will answer either "yes," "no" or "wait."

God promises an answer to prayer. His answer might be "Yes." Or, it might be "Wait," or even "No."

The important fact to remember is that God gave both of you life, and on your wedding day you both made your vows to Him that you would live together till death separates you. Then we must we trust—placing all our needs and cares on Jesus. It is understanding that neither I nor my spouse can believe in Jesus or come to Him, only through faith which comes through the Word.

Again, read what the Bible tells us in Romans 10:17, *"Consequently, faith comes from hearing the message, and the message is heard through the Word of Christ."* When both spouses understand this, each one is able to forgive and respect each other as a forgiven child of God.

When a person can look inside his or her own heart, and when the spouse can recognize the shortcomings and failures that can only be removed through faith in Jesus Christ who took the sins of the whole world to the cross and paid for them, every failure, no matter how great or how small, then each one can look at the other in a different way. A way that says I know you are not perfect, I know you make mistakes, but I know that I do also and just as Christ has forgiven me, I forgive you.

It is only when we are able to sincerely say (and believe in our hearts), "I know you are not perfect, I know you make mistakes, but I know that I do also and just as Christ has forgiven me, I forgive you." that reconciliation can happen.

I may not like what you have said or what you have done to me and to our family, but I can forgive you.

You may not like what I have said, how I have acted, and what I have done to you and to our family but you can forgive me.

The two paragraphs you just read are to help the reader understand again that it is not just your spouse who needs help but also you, and when you look at yourself and what you can do to save your marriage, it is then that progress is beginning to take place.

Now when each spouse is willing to abide by God's command and make their marriage work, what are the expectations and concerns they face? We will take a look at some of the challenges faced by Sarah and Alan as they started their new beginnings.

A New Beginning

Sarah related she was very nervous about moving back to their home with Alan since it had not been sold and they had decided to keep it. The day before Alan moved her and Alan, Jr. back to their home, their pastor had arranged a counseling and planning session. He offered a plan for them and asked them to agree to as follows:

1. Get up each morning and begin the day with prayer. This is the prayer he asked them to pray together.

   "Dear Heavenly Father, we thank You for protection and restful sleep this past night. Help us face this day in the sure knowledge that You will be with us and that You will protect our family from all harm and danger. Help us to grow in love for You and love for each other. Bless our marriage and our family. In Jesus' name. Amen."

2. Do not expect your love to be the way it was in the beginning. Remember—you are two adults who fell in love and problems came into your marriage because each of you did not measure up to the other's expectations.

3. Work at being good friends and being kind and considerate of one another.

4. Attend Bible Class and Church every Sunday.

5. Plan on a social night out together at least once per month. It may be just going to a restaurant for the evening meal and a movie. Try to make this a pleasant time with good conversation. This may be awkward at first but just do it and trust each other to make it work.

6. Before you go to bed each night have a 15 minute devotion together. An example could be for Alan to open with a brief prayer such as,

"O Lord, we thank You for this day. Most of all we thank You for sending Your Son, Jesus Christ, to be our Savior who gives us eternal life through His death on the cross. We are Your children and we ask You to give us restful sleep. Bless Alan, Jr. and keep us all in Your tender loving care. Lord, help us grow each day as we look to You to make our family grow stronger. In Jesus' name. Amen."

Sarah and Alan have three months under their belts with this plan and are meeting with their pastor. Both Sarah and Alan and their pastor say they believe progress is being made. All three know that they must be patient knowing there are still problems that must be faced. But this couple and their pastor are examples of what should be done when there is a serious problem between spouses.

A New Beginning

We live in a sinful and imperfect world, and we receive all kinds of mixed signals from a society that does not look to God our Creator for guidance and direction.

Instead we look to self. Dissatisfaction with our marriage, our in-laws, our families or our role in life can lead us into self-pity and loss of self-worth. All of this affects our dealings with our spouse and what we expect from our relationship.

How do we get help? Think for one moment of all the blessings of medicine we have today. What would happen if your doctor prescribed a medicine for a serious infection that you have, you go to the pharmacy and your pharmacist tells you all about how good the medication is and how it works for someone with your problem and then you do not buy the medicine? You could deceive yourself, saying, "I can get this on my own. I can do it myself."

How very foolish one would be to act in this way! Yet when we face problems in our marriage, a vow till death parts us, we often run away from the one true healing source and look for secular ways of healing or ending the marriage rather than turning to the only source that will not fail us as we read, study and do according to God's Holy Word. We read in Jeremiah 30:17, *"But I will restore you to health and heal your wounds, declares the Lord."*

There is one true source to heal the hurts in our lives—to read, study and do according to God's Word.

Sarah and Alan took this route and as God's children recognized that it was their responsibility to use the resources that God provided for them. Always use the proper resources if you want to get the proper results.

Marriage Is for Life!

In healing a broken marriage the proper resources are:

1. God's Word - II Timothy 3:16, "*All Scripture is God-breathed and is useful for teaching, rebuking, correcting and training in righteousness.*"

2. The Pastor - who knows God's Word and how to help both spouses apply it as His forgiven and redeemed children. He can help each spouse see God's mercy in their lives and how to apply it to their marriage.

However, the couple must hear and heed the pastor's counsel and both are responsible to seek the pastor's help and guidance. Now that you have read this chapter please take a few minutes to turn to the journal pages and write down your thoughts, using the questions provided as guides.

Three Things to Remember

✴ Remember your two most
  important resources for healing
  and growth: God's Word and
  your pastor, who knows God's
  Word and can help you apply it
  in your marriage and your life.

✴ You cannot do it alone. Admit
  this to yourself and allow yourself to accept help and guidance
  from God and your pastor.

✴ God has already forgiven us all.
  You can forgive your spouse,
  even if you do not like or agree
  with what your mate has said
  or done to you and your family.

Three Things to Do

❊ Meet with your pastor and develop a mutually agreed upon contract to guide you as you make your new beginning. The samples on page 105 and 121 can be used as guides.

❊ Read Jeremiah 16 with your mate. Discuss what this message means to you.

❊ Plan a special night out to celebrate your new beginning.

Couple's Journal—For Her

Why should any marriage be saved?

What meaning does God's Word have for my life?

How can our marriage be saved?

What is marriage?

....

....

....

....

....

....

....

....

....

....

....

....

....

....

....

Couple's Journal–For Him

Why should any marriage be saved?

What meaning does God's Word have for my life?

How can our marriage be saved?

What is marriage?

....

....

....

....

....

....

....

....

....

....

....

....

....

....

❧ Chapter 7 ❧

Lo, I Am With You, Each Day at a Time

As the reader looks at this chapter it is my hope that a feeling of trust, hope, self-worth and anticipation can begin to grow in each spouse as you commit to make your first marriage pledge to God to continue "till death do us part."

In Matthew 28:20b when Jesus sent His disciples out to proclaim what it meant to trust in Him, He told them and all who believe in Him, *"And surely I am with you always, to the very end of the age."*

Now what is so important for one to understand is that when we put our trust in Him, He says very simply, "I am with you," and that means help for each spouse as they struggle to heal their hurting marriage, their so-called shattered dream.

God wants us to understand very well that the shattering took place when Adam and Eve disobeyed Him. A perfect marriage ended when Adam and Eve were put out of the Garden of Eden. Man and woman went from perfect to

A perfect marriage ended when Adam and Eve were put out of the Garden of Eden, yet we have His promise, "I am with you."

imperfect, and because of this, sin entered the world. If you do not know what this word—sin— means, then find out from someone who knows.

The Bible tells us very simply that it is disobedience to our Creator God, a God who loved His people so much that when they disobeyed Him, He provided a way for them and all people to come back into a right relationship with Him, our God and Creator. God made the promise that He would send a Savior, His Son, to free mankind, yes, all people, from their disobedience and their sin of rebellion.

What God has joined together in this marriage can certainly be healed if the desire and trust in Him are there.

As a spouse looks to healing a marriage, trust is absolutely necessary in the healing process. The trust based in the fact that a loving God, who sent His Son to pay for all sins, will help a couple who trusts in Him to give them the guidance, the strength and the courage to overcome the material difficulties they are facing. What God has joined together in this marriage can certainly be healed if the desire and trust in Him are there.

He says, "Lo, I am with you always." Hurting spouses need to ask what this means. It means that somehow, someway, the secular world has gotten into the marriage and that happens when priorities get out of the proper order.

When I say I trust in God and His Son, Jesus Christ, as my Savior, then it follows that my spouse and I have Him first in our marriage and that means going to church EVERY Sunday where our faith will grow. You have read these words before, but they are worth emphasizing again, from the book of Romans, where God tells us, *"Consequently, faith comes from hearing* the message, and the message is heard through the Word of Christ."

When we trust Him, we can begin to trust each other. When I trust my spouse, it means that I trust myself. It means I have good feelings about myself, and that can only come when I understand the word MERCY.

When we fully trust in God, we can trust ourselves, our spouse and can fully comprehend His mercy to us.

What does mercy mean? Simply, mercy is the forgiving love of God as shown to us in Christ, who was completely sinless, and took our sins on Himself. When I as an individual realize how much mercy God has shown me, I trust that He will give me the understanding to show mercy and that means being able to forgive my spouse.

If I can forgive my spouse as the Lord has forgiven me, I can work for a new and proper relationship in our marriage. Titus 3:4-5a defines real mercy in these words, *"But when the kindness and love of God our Savior appeared, He saved us, not because of righteous things we had done, but because of His mercy."*

Now it follows that if a couple understands God's mercy and if they can look at each other in the knowledge and trust of what God has done for them, it is then possible for a trust that has been shattered and broken to be mended and made right again when each spouse trusts in God's Holy Word and promises.

Christ Himself tells us again what is expected of each spouse in Ephesians 5:21, *"Submit to one another out of reverence for Christ."* In this same chapter, Ephesians 5:31, *"For this reason a man will leave his father and mother and be united to his wife, and the two will become one flesh."*

There is a solution to the problems that you and your spouse are facing. When you trust in Him, there is hope.

Trust comes about when each spouse trusts God and because of that trust a NEW trust can be established because of what God can do when we are unable to and trust in Him. *"Lo, I am with you always."* Our Bible assures us in Jeremiah 23:23, *"'Am I only a God nearby,' declares the Lord, 'and not a God far away?'"*

The point is, He is always there when the need is felt. The need is there when a marriage begins to get into trouble. There is a solution to the problems that you and your spouse are facing. When you trust in Him, there is hope.

Mary had this to say about hope. "When I was a little girl I remember hoping for a special part in our Christmas program at church. I remember as a teenager hoping that I would make the cheerleading squad, and I remember my hope chest as my mother and I put different special items in it for when I met that special one in my life.

"In our family as I grew up with my brother and sister, hope was something we were taught. We looked to the future with hope. We were taught that our sure hope was in Jesus Christ and that we could, and should, cast all of our cares on Him.

Don't let the gossip of "well-meaning" friends create suspicion and friction between you and your spouse.

"During my teenage years hope in Jesus carried me through some difficult times. When I began college, I hoped that I would meet the right guy for me. I knew I had that lifetime partner when I met Bill one night in the library. He had blond, curly hair, big blue eyes and was so friendly. Within six months Bill and I were married. He was a Senior and I was a Sophomore.

"Both of our parents urged us to wait. No way would we wait! I was hoping for the perfect marriage. We rented a two bedroom apartment near the campus. Our plan was for me to work while Bill finished his degree in teaching, then I would finish my degree. He was getting his degree in high school Physical Education, and he wanted to coach girl's basketball.

"When Bill graduated we had hoped he would get a school near the college we were attending, since I had a good job in the college bookstore and hoped that I could continue part time while I finished my degree and Bill taught. During Bill's senior year he sent out resumes to all the high schools near the campus but none of them needed a physical education teacher/basketball coach.

"By graduation time he had only one feeler and that school hired one of Bill's classmates. In August we had decided that Bill would get a job with the campus Maintenance Department. Then a small district in a rural community 300 miles away offered him a physical education position as well as head coach for the girl's basketball team. It was just the kind of opportunity Bill had been hoping for, but we knew the salary was not great.

"I would be too far away from a university to finish my degree. Although we were brought up as Christians and went to Sunday School and church and were married in my church, our lives had been so busy we just had not been active in church since we got married. I told Bill we should pray about this offer and then make a decision.

"Bill smiled and said, 'O.K., as long as we make the move.' Needless to say we made the move. I really was afraid it was the wrong move but knew it was what Bill wanted. I hoped that it would work out. We agreed that I would work and my degree would be delayed for the time being.

"We moved into a nice two bedroom apartment near the high school and Bill started his duties. I was lucky and got a job at the local bank as a teller. Things seemed to be working out for us. Bill was pleased with his classes and he had the potential for a decent basketball team.

"And then you can guess what happened next. A "slip-up"—morning sickness, not a good time in our lives for a baby to come along. Bill was furious. I wanted a baby but not now. However, we accepted the fact and agreed we would cope.

"The plan was for me to work as long as possible and our parents would help. As I look back now, I began to lose hope—morning sickness was horrible. It lasted almost all day. I never felt good one day during my pregnancy, and Bill had no sympathy as I saw it. His classes and his girls' team took first priority, and I was getting left behind with a growing stomach. Things were not looking good, and then one of my friends crushed me with the concern that Bill was showing too much attention to his assistant coach, who was single and very pretty.

"I was devastated, my hopes and dreams shattered. God, where are You, why is this happening to me?

"My friend had shared this with me on a Wednesday when we had agreed to meet for lunch. I could not go back to work. I went home and cried all afternoon. When Bill came in he knew right away something was wrong. I blurted it out, 'How could you do this to me? I am carrying your baby, you married me, you pledged to me till death do us part, what kind of jerk are you? I want a divorce now!'

Lo, I Am With You, Each Day at a Time

"After much talking and spending time with our pastor we were able to work things out and here is the way we were able to get our marriage on track. We agreed to a contract that Pastor set up and the contract that we both signed is as follows:

1. We must attend church and Adult Bible Class every Sunday

2. We must spend 30 minutes reading and discussing the Bible together in devotions at least five evenings per week

3. We must spend one hour each month with pastor

4. Talking time when just the two us share the good things and the challenges that are happening to us

5. Each day we will pray for each other that God will guide and direct us in our marriage

"We both signed the contract on a Wednesday evening a little over a year ago. I was desperate. I knew I still loved Bill but I was very doubtful about the contract and Bill.

"The author of this book can tell the rest of my story."

Mary and Bill have a baby boy named Bill, Jr. Since the signing of the contract their marriage has improved. They are living up to the contract and both feel that real progress is being made. Both say there have been trying days when mistakes have been made, but in talking with them you can feel a real pride in their "making it."

There is a real respect for each other and as Mary says, "I have my hope back and it comes from God who brought us together and expects us to stay together till death separates us."

When we look at Bill and Mary's experience, we are able to understand that God's people are not perfect, that mistakes are made, feelings are hurt, dreams shattered and hope lost. But when individual spouses are willing to recognize God as the real authority in life, a failing marriage can be saved.

When the man and woman are willing to listen to Him who loved them and gave Himself for them, a new hope can take the place of gloom and doom. And that is just what took place with Mary and Bill, thanks to a wise and loving pastor who would not give in to divorce but told them the real truth that divorce was unacceptable in God's sight and that they had to work it out.

When a marriage is in trouble, it means that one or both partners have moved away or never really had the proper relationship with God and without that, there is no lasting hope for a marriage or a happy family.

Holy Scripture tells us in Lamentations 3:25-26, *"The Lord is good to those whose hope is in Him, to the one who seeks Him; it is good to wait quietly for the salvation of the Lord."*

I believe what put Bill and Mary back on the right track for a happy and secure marriage was the simple fact that both of them were willing to listen to what God was telling them through His Word.

When a marriage is in trouble, it means that one or both partners have moved away or never really had the proper relationship with God and without that, there is no lasting hope for a marriage or a happy family.

Lo, I Am With You, Each Day at a Time

Recently a man and woman about 40 years of age came into my office for help. Both agreed that they loved each other and that they wanted their marriage to be saved, but to save it they needed counseling. Everything was fine until I indicated that a closer relationship with God, that could only come through the Word, which meant church, Bible Class and home devotions, was necessary.

The man got up and walked out. Their divorce is going to be final, no contest, just a friendly divorce. How tragic! Their promises broken and their dreams shattered. And the Lord says to each person, *"Lo, I want to be with you each day at a time."* It is a sure promise that He will be there for us when He is a part of our life. He wants to be a part of your marriage. He wants to heal the hurt. There is real help. There is real hope.

Reflect on the stories in this chapter, and think about how you feel today about your life, marriage and relationship with God. Think about the word—HOPE—and what it really means to have hope for a better tomorrow. Use the journal pages to record your thoughts and feelings.

Three Things to Remember

* Trust in Jesus. He can give you real hope.

* God promises to be with you always.

* A happy and secure marriage is founded in faith and trust in God and His promises to us.

Three Things to Do

❋ Have a conversation with your spouse about trust.

❋ Memorize a Bible verse that speaks to you about hope, trust or God's promise to be with you. Share the verse with your mate.

❋ Every day pray for your marriage, your spouse and yourself.

Couple's Journal–For Her

What is hope?

How can a pastor help you?

What does your marriage need every day?

What does your spouse need the most?

How does God love you?

....

....

....

....

....

....

....

....

....

....

....

....

....

....

Couple's Journal—For Him

What is hope?

How can a pastor help you?

What does your marriage need every day?

What does your spouse need the most?

How does God love you?

....

....

....

....

....

....

....

....

....

....

....

....

....

❈ Chapter 8 ❈
Running Together

Ihave titled this chapter of my book *Running Together* because I have always admired a relay team, each member very capable but dependent on the rest of the team if they are going to win the race. I see a successful marriage and family the same way.

God gives each individual special gifts that make him or her a unique individual. Even identical twins are different. When a man and woman fall in love, two unique individuals come together, each different but now one.

For the marriage to be successful, out of this oneness must come a mutual trust, a free and open communication, a desire to please one another as one's self wants to be pleased, feel wanted, needed and important, a giving of one's self, unconditionally, to the other. When the two react in this way to each other, a wonderful and beautiful race is being run.

The world and society today would have us believe that marriage is not a lifetime commitment but a convenience that can be used as long

A good marriage, like a successful relay team, runs together—each individual capable and competent, yet still dependent upon his or her partner if they are to succeed.

as it is convenient, but can be discarded at the whim of one or both partners.

When the family team starts to malfunction and is torn apart, children of every age suffer because of this. Teen suicide and drug and alcohol abuse are the leading killers of our youth because they feel unloved, unwanted and with no real purpose in their lives.

Any couple contemplating divorce must take a hard look within and ask soul-searching questions, "What can I do? How can I save my marriage and the family for which God has made me responsible as part of my marriage team? How can my spouse and I, as God's redeemed children, run the race He called us to run when we became one in His sight?"

The question should not be "Can we?" Because of the fact that we are His children and because we know that we can do all things through Jesus Christ, we know that we can and we will make our marriage work. We will run together. We will use the tools that are available to make our marriage work.

It is not advanced technology or superior teaching methodology that creates a successful student. It is being brought up in the love and nurture of a Christian home, regular attendance at worship and dedication to applying God's Word in our everyday lives.

There are many helps that God has provided when, because of a variety of reasons, a marriage gets into trouble. Do you know what the most important factors are for a child to succeed in school? In today's world, with all its advanced teaching technology, all the well-rounded curriculums, a recent survey shows that a highly successful high school student is one who:

1. Comes from a two-parent family and is shown by example the parents' love for each other and their children.

2. Has been taught a work ethic
3. Has a high degree of self-confidence as a result of the home environment which was nurtured by both parents

4. Is well disciplined and understands consequences and accountability which is the result of two parents who support each other in their discipline

5. Believes, as a result of being exposed by mom and dad to church and Sunday School, what the Bible teaches and means for every individual according to Acts 4:12, *"Salvation is found in no one else, for there is no other name under heaven given to men by which we must be saved."*

The Holy Bible in Romans 10:17 also tells us as parents how our saving faith comes to us and our children, *"Consequently, faith comes from hearing the message, and the message is heard through the Word of Christ."*

Families are as strong as their bond is to God our Heavenly Father. This bond is kept strong through the Holy Spirit working through Word and Sacrament, which keeps faith in our one and only Savior, Jesus Christ.

In running together, when the marriage is on track, what makes it strong and keeps it strong in a society that has lost many of its traditional values?

Marriage Is for Life!

Devotional time provides strength to your marriage and peace and quiet for your soul. Set aside time each and every day to communicate with God in prayer.

One thing is to make sure that both spouses agree to a time each day for prayer and family devotions. I suggest getting up 30 minutes earlier in the morning and let that devotion time start your day. You can be absolutely sure that in your daily devotion time and in these moments of worship together lie the strength of your marriage and the peace and quiet for your souls.

For a marriage to continue safe and secure it is vitally important that the partners, with Christ in their marriage, listen to our God of peace as they begin each day. He loves each one of you in this family arrangement that He made with you when you made your marriage vows.

While we live in this world we will no doubt always have to put up with challenges that come from our partner, our children, all being imperfect because of sin, but there is a guaranteed remedy. The remedy is the Lord Jesus Christ.

The remedy to all the challenges in our day, big or small, lies in our Lord and Savior, Jesus Christ.

Listen how He gives each spouse and each member of the family this assurance in John 14:27, *"Peace I leave with you; My peace I give you. I do not give to you as the world gives. Do not let your hearts be troubled and do not be afraid."* His Word of peace to you that is unbreakable is found in Psalm 46:10a, *"Be still, and know that I am God."*

When a marriage is functioning according to God's will, the children in that family are content as the family runs together. The violence and other problems that children are facing today are mainly a result of mother and father not functioning together as a unit.

The following is an example of what can happen to a well-adjusted family when a marriage begins

134

to break down. All through school until the beginning of fourth grade, Missy was a happy, well-adjusted little girl. Then her teacher, Mrs. Johnson started to notice some minor behavior problems that continued to grow more serious every week. Mrs. Johnson, in consultation with her principal, asked for a conference with the parents.

In preparation for the conference Mrs. Johnson listed some of her concerns: Missy was changing from a very outgoing happy little girl to one who cried because her best friends would not let her be "in charge," so to speak. She tried to play one friend against the other. She would do things to get special attention from her teacher.

Missy had gone from a very nice and polite little girl to a very withdrawn, demanding and temperamental little girl. Her homework and school work in general was beginning to suffer.

When Missy's mother came in for the conference she was alone and explained that her husband was unable to make the conference. When Missy's teacher explained her concerns to the mother, she began to cry and indicated there was a problem between her and Missy's father.

Mrs. Johnson encouraged counseling and help from their pastor. The good news is that Missy's parents recognized that a little girl was having problems because a mommy and daddy were having problems. They had let their marriage lose its priority and mother, father and Missy were starting to suffer.

When these two parents saw how their child, this gift from God, was hurting because of them and their actions toward each other, they went to their pastor and asked for help. Their pastor was able to help them focus on what their responsibility was to each other and their child.

They realized there was something they were beginning to lose or forget, "till death do us part, in sickness or health, in good times or bad."

Because of a willingness to listen to what God has to say and what they knew was right, this marriage is healing and a little girl is starting to be the secure happy little girl she once was.

It is the same for children of any age. When a marriage starts to fail, no matter what the age, the child or children start to have problems of insecurity. They can lose their self-worth and blame themselves for mom and dad's problems.

A sixteen-year-old boy told me of the struggles and fears of the last day in his elementary school. "My father lived in Florida and I was with my mom in Michigan. I had to go to Florida to visit my father and then it would be decided where I was to go to high school. What a bummer for me! I loved my mom and dad both. I wanted us to be a family. I wondered if it was me that caused the divorce. They both say 'no' but I do know that I heard them argue about me. The three of us were at one time really happy together. But now life is not good for me."

More teenagers give up hope because mom and dad let their marriage fall apart, and many of these young children of tomorrow never reach adulthood. Drugs and suicide end their lives.

Children at an early age need to know that there is real hope for them. They need to be able to trust the adults in their lives. They need to know and feel secure that mom and dad love them equally. They need to feel that they belong to a mother and father who love them, each one of them for whom they are. They need to feel they are family and running the race of life together.

When you and your spouse said your marriage vows, you pledged to God that you wanted to run together for the rest of your life in His world and that if He blessed you with children, you would bring them up for Him. As a great reformer said in speaking to society, "God did not give you your children and the means to support them simply so that you may do with them just as you please, or train them just to get ahead in the world. You have been earnestly commanded to raise them for God's service."

We need to recognize that many parents are unwilling to sacrifice for their children. What parents must understand is that they are setting examples as they always have done, and children do not need to see selfishness from mom and dad.

What they do need to see is firm love, a love that shows unity in purpose from mom and dad. Wise parents, when the family is running together, know there is a time to work, a time to play, a time to be a parent and a time to be a family.

Children watch the way their parents live their lives. If they like what they see, if it makes sense to them, they will live their lives that way too.

In most marriages, having a child is the easy part. Bringing one up to be a good citizen is a commitment by both parents. Every generation has moved ahead on the basis of the training it received from the past. There is no alternative to the role each parent has in building a society that has sound values.

Marriage Is for Life!

Over and over we see that marriage is made for life for each other and for the children. God wants every marriage to be for life. Every person, every counselor and every pastor should know that absolutely no marriage can be so bad, no family so torn that it cannot be repaired. This is for sure and certain, revealed to us by the one and only True God through His Holy Scriptures. This is His promise to us—that He loves the world in general and He loves and cares for each one of us individually.

Now this Lord of all creation says to you in Isaiah 43:1b, *"Fear not, for I have redeemed you; I have summoned you by name; you are Mine."* God deeply cares about you and your partner and about your children as you run together as His family.

When each person in the family can read His truth from Holy Scripture and when each spouse approaches marriage with these very special and beautiful truths in mind, we can solve family problems the way God wants us to.

We read in Galatians 2:20, *"I have been crucified with Christ and I no longer live, but Christ lives in me. The life I live in the body, I live by faith in the Son of God, who loved me and gave Himself for me."* He tells each man, woman and child in Psalm 50:15, *"Call upon Me in the day of trouble; I will deliver you, and you will honor Me."*

Every marriage has challenges but when each spouse realizes what God wants and expects of them in their marriage, the marriage can and will be for life.

Marriage Is for Life

Three Things to Remember

❋ There must be a mutual trust between husband and wife.

❋ Each person must feel needed and wanted.

❋ Church, Sunday school and family devotions.

Three Things to Do

* Spend time together in an exercise program.

* Make family devotions a must.

* Join a support group or start one at your church—for seniors, teens or adults in need.

A Note to Couples Considering Marriage

This entire book can be a helpful resource to couples considering marriage. It can be used during premarital sessions with your pastor to help you understand and apply God's plan for marriage. It is absolutely a must for any person to consider the following when they have fallen in love.

Engagement should be for at least one year. During the engagement period the couple should spend a great deal of time discussing their compatibility for a lifetime together. There are some "to do's" and "not to do's" if a Christian young man and woman desire to beat the statistics and spend a lifetime together.

One of the most important factors in a lasting marriage is for the two partners to be of the same faith. To try to resolve this issue later on or to say this issue will not matter is setting the marriage up for trouble in the future. Resolve this conflict prior to the marriage vows. Be practical. This is the most important decision about your life and future that the two of you will make.

The second most important part of your planning a lifetime together is no sex before the marriage vows. "What?" you might say, "Why how dumb and old fashioned can you be?"

Do not be fooled by the world's standards. If your marriage is to last, make sure you are living according to God's standards. His Word has not changed. The Sixth Commandment tells us that adultery should not be committed and when sex takes place before marriage, both partners are cheapened. If you are living together, stop and seek forgiveness. When people live together without marriage, they are sinning against God. Sooner or later problems begin to plague the couple. Do not get caught in this trap.

As you plan for your future together you must decide who will take care of the finances. Oftentimes financial problems are the beginning of real material problems.

Regular attendance in church must be agreed upon before the vows are said. Should God bless you with that special blessing of children, they must be brought up in the house of the Lord.

If a couple cannot commit to these expectations that come from God, they should seriously consider the fact that they may not be meant for a lifetime together as husband and wife.

If You've Already Divorced

This book was written to help heal a troubled marriage, but you may be someone who has already divorced. "What is there for me?" you might be asking. "I can't heal my marriage—my spouse is gone." Where there is true repentance, there is forgiveness, and you can still have hope for a better tomorrow.

If you, reader were married and because of this sinful world in which we live, Satan has been able to cause your spouse to break the vows made before God or if you have tried in every way to make the marriage work, but your partner has committed adultery and refuses to repent and live up to what God tells us to do, or if your spouse has deserted you through abuse or refuses to honor you, love you and keep you in sickness or in health, then you are free to divorce with no guilt and no remorse.

You must start a new life as you continue in God your Heavenly Father who has called you out of darkness into His marvelous light.

And His promise to you is, "Lo, I am with you always."

Sources of Help

❈ Counsel with your pastor. He is your friend and confidant. Both spouses must have a support group.

❈ Talk with an older person who has lived through the joys and trials of a successful marriage.

❈ Seek help from a Christian counselor who understands that marriage is for a lifetime.

❈ If you are planning to be married, plan for at least six months of pre-marital counseling—and listen to what the counselor has to say!

A Special Seminar for Families. . .
The Christian Family Today

The Christian Family Today seminar was developed to help families from all walks of life take a closer look at what goes into a healthy family relationship.

Whether you are experiencing difficulties with your spouse or children, or want to make a good relationship even better, this seminar will provide you with practical helps that you can put to use right away.

What role does "self esteem" play in building a strong family? Will discipline damage my child's self-esteem? What causes marital breakdown, and what can be done to heal hurting relationships?

When is divorce an option? What is the role of the church in building a strong family? Is forgiveness "for real?" These are just a few of the questions that are discussed in The Christian Family Today.

The Seminar is led by the Rev. Albert B. Wingfield, author of *Marriage Is for Life—No Broken Promises,* *No Shattered Dreams.* Rev. Wingfield is a dynamic speaker who has the experience to back it up! Currently Vice President of Business Affairs at Concordia Theological Seminary, Fort Wayne, Indiana, Rev. Wingfield has also served in several Lutheran schools as teacher, dean of students, principal, headmaster and superintendent.

Parents of six children, Rev. Wingfield and his wife Marge have, over the years, also opened their home to numerous foster children, international students, elderly family members, and are now happy in their role as devoted grandparents.

There is much talk in the media about the "breakdown" in today's society and the decay of moral responsibility and values. What role can the Church play in supporting and nurturing families?

Rev. Wingfield will share his vision for implementing an "extended family" within the church, and restoring the church to a more central position in building up and upholding the family.

Guest speakers bring their own experiences in dealing with a variety of family situations. You will learn what to expect in situations such as divorce, loss of a spouse or loved one, what to do with aging parents, troubled children and teens, and ensure your family's financial future.

The seminar offers opportunities for discussion and role-playing, as well as the traditional "lecture" style presentation. Ample time is provided for questions and interaction between speakers and seminar participants. Each seminar is unique, based on input from those who have registered.

Seminar Topics Include:

- Marriage
- Career Stress
- Children
- Aging Parents
- Single Parenting
- Schooling
- Teens
- Discipline
- Worship
- What should you expect from your church?
- What should your church expect from you?

For information on the date and location of the seminar nearest you, or to host a seminar at your church, contact Rev. Al Wingfield, CTS Family Press • 6600 North Clinton Street • Fort Wayne, IN 46825.

Telephone: (219)452-2106   Fax: (219)452-2121
Email: wingfieldab@mail.ctsfw.edu

CTS Family Press
Sharing the message of God's love!

You can share God's message of hope and love with others, too. Complete the enclosed order form to request copies for your pastor, family and friends, copies for mission congregations and shut-ins, or to make a financial contribution. Thank You!

Adults and Teens

Marriage Is for Life
No Broken Promises, No Shattered Dreams

This book is a "must have" for everyone who is married, engaged, or counseling couples. Topics are addressed in a clear, down-to-earth style, with Bible-based guidance that is easy to read and understand. **$9.99**

Going Home Talk

A wonderful devotional for Christians of all ages, Pastor Skibbe's relaxed style encourages readers and leads them on a journey towards their heavenly home. Large print spiral bound format is ideal for seniors, or for reading aloud. **$13.50**

Children

The Little Snail That Lives Near a Pail

This charming story features a four-year-old girl who wonders, "Who made the little snail?" Color photos throughout add interest and appeal to a story that any preschooler is sure to love. **$7.95**

Come! See! With Little Becky Ann (Coming Jan 2000)

Becky Ann goes for a walk with her dad and is excited to show him everything she sees. From worms and honeybees to puppies, kittens, and Becky Ann herself, this winsome girl learns that God made everything, and loves every bit of His creation. **$7.95**

The Twins in the Green Forest (Coming Jan 2000)

Micah and Marsall explore the woods near their home. What will they see? Who will they meet? These five-year-old twins have a contagious enthusiasm and curiosity that will have kids smiling and asking to hear this story again and again. **$7.95**

CTS FAMILY PRESS—Sharing the message of God's Love

YES! I want to help CTS Press share the message of God's love.
Enclosed is my gift of:

- ☐ $25
- ☐ $100
- ☐ $500
- ☐ $50
- ☐ $250
- ☐ Other _____

☐ Please donate my purchase to mission congregations or shut-ins.
☐ Please contact me about your Today's Family Seminar

Name: _____

Address: _____

City: _____

State/Zip: _____   Phone: _____

Title	Price	Qty.	Total
Marriage Is for Life	$9.99		
Going Home Talk	$13.50		
The Little Snail That Lives Near a Pail	$7.95		
Come! See! With Little Becky Ann	$7.95		
The Twins in the Green Forest	$7.95		
		Order Total	

Payment Options:

☐ My check is enclosed   ☐ Please charge my ☐ VISA ☐ Mastercard.

Card No: _____   Expiration Date: _____

Please make checks payable to Concordia Theological Seminary, and return with your order form to CTS Press • 6600 North Clinton Street • Fort Wayne, IN 46825

CTS FAMILY PRESS—Sharing the message of God's Love

YES! I want to help CTS Press share the message of God's love.
Enclosed is my gift of:

- ☐ $25
- ☐ $100
- ☐ $500
- ☐ $50
- ☐ $250
- ☐ Other _____

☐ Please donate my purchase to mission congregations or shut-ins.
☐ Please contact me about your Today's Family Seminar

Name: _____

Address: _____

City: _____

State/Zip: _____   Phone: _____

Title	Price	Qty.	Total
Marriage Is for Life	$9.99		
Going Home Talk	$13.50		
The Little Snail That Lives Near a Pail	$7.95		
Come! See! With Little Becky Ann	$7.95		
The Twins in the Green Forest	$7.95		
		Order Total	

Payment Options:

☐ My check is enclosed   ☐ Please charge my ☐ VISA ☐ Mastercard.

Card No: _____   Expiration Date: _____

Please make checks payable to Concordia Theological Seminary, and return with your order form to CTS Press • 6600 North Clinton Street • Fort Wayne, IN 46825

CTS FAMILY PRESS—Sharing the message of God's Love

Title	Price	Qty.	Total
Marriage Is for Life	$9.99		
Going Home Talk	$13.50		
The Little Snail That Lives Near a Pail	$7.95		
Come! See! With Little Becky Ann	$7.95		
The Twins in the Green Forest	$7.95		
		Order Total	

Payment Options:

☐ My check is enclosed   ☐ Please charge my ☐ VISA ☐ Mastercard.

Card No: _____ Expiration Date: _____

Please make checks payable to Concordia Theological Seminary, and return with your order form to CTS Press • 6600 North Clinton Street • Fort Wayne, IN 46825

YES! I want to help CTS Press share the message of God's love.
Enclosed is my gift of:

☐ $25   ☐ $100   ☐ $500
☐ $50   ☐ $250   ☐ Other _____

☐ Please donate my purchase to mission congregations or shut-ins.
☐ Please contact me about your Today's Family Seminar

Name: _____
Address: _____
City: _____
State/Zip: _____ Phone: _____

CTS FAMILY PRESS—Sharing the message of God's Love

Title	Price	Qty.	Total
Marriage Is for Life	$9.99		
Going Home Talk	$13.50		
The Little Snail That Lives Near a Pail	$7.95		
Come! See! With Little Becky Ann	$7.95		
The Twins in the Green Forest	$7.95		
		Order Total	

Payment Options:

☐ My check is enclosed   ☐ Please charge my ☐ VISA ☐ Mastercard.

Card No: _____ Expiration Date: _____

Please make checks payable to Concordia Theological Seminary, and return with your order form to CTS Press • 6600 North Clinton Street • Fort Wayne, IN 46825

YES! I want to help CTS Press share the message of God's love.
Enclosed is my gift of:

☐ $25   ☐ $100   ☐ $500
☐ $50   ☐ $250   ☐ Other _____

☐ Please donate my purchase to mission congregations or shut-ins.
☐ Please contact me about your Today's Family Seminar

Name: _____
Address: _____
City: _____
State/Zip: _____ Phone: _____